Stepping Out

Stepping Out

The Golden Age
of Montreal Night Clubs
1925 - 1955

Nancy Marrelli

Véhicule Press

MONTRÉAL

Published with the generous assistance of the Book Publishing Industry Development Program of the Department of Canadian Heritage, and the Société de développement des entreprises culturelles du Québec (SODEC).

Cover and interior design by J.W. Stewart
Maps by Oisin Little of Little Animation Inc.
Front and back cover images are from the Concordia University Archives.
Front cover: Mynie Sutton scrapbook. *Back cover:* Mynie Sutton scrapbook, Joe Bell scrapbook, Herb Johnson fonds, Al Palmer fonds
Printed by AGMV-Marquis Inc.

Library and Archives Canada Cataloguing in Publication

Marrelli, Nancy
Stepping out : the golden age of Montreal night clubs / Nancy Marrelli.

Materials from the Montreal jazz collection at the Concordia University Archives.
Includes index.
ISBN 1-55065-193-5

1. Nightclubs--Québec (Province)--Montréal--History--20th century.
I. Concordia University. Archives II. Title.

FC2947.63.M37 2004   792.7'0971428'0904   C2004-904022-7

Véhicule Press
www.vehiculepress.com

Canadian Distribution: LitDistCo, 100 Armstrong Avenue,
Georgetown, Ontario, L7G 5S4 / 800-591-6250 / orders@litdistco.ca

U.S. Distribution: Independent Publishers Group, 814 North Franklin Street,
Chicago, Illinois 60610 / 800-888-4741 / frontdesk@ipgbook.com / www.ipgbook.com

Printed in Canada

Contents

PREFACE

In the 1980s Concordia University Archives began acquiring and preserving materials on Montreal jazz history at the suggestion of John Gilmore. He is the author of *Swinging in Paradise: The Story of Jazz in Montreal* (1988) and *Who's Who of Jazz in Montreal: Ragtime to 1970* (1989), both published by Véhicule Press. With the collaboration of Concordia's Music Department, the Archives continues to acquire materials that document Montreal jazz musicians and the Montreal night scene in which they performed.

The Archives has a wide range of materials on Montreal jazz and night life, including photographs, recordings, scrapbooks, posters, swizzle sticks, menus, press clippings, music scores, sheet music, correspondence, oral history recordings, and other items. This documentation has been used by hundreds of researchers for purposes that would have seemed unimaginable to the people who collected and protected the material before it came to the Archives. The materials have been generously donated by the families of musicians Myron Sutton, Joe Bell, Herb Johnson, Henry Whiston, Roland Lavallée, Gordie Fleming, and by individuals such as John Gilmore, Alex Robertson, Johnny Holmes, Vic Vogel, Tina Brereton, Meilan Lam, Andrew Homzy, Bob Redmond, Norma Morara Hayes, and many others. These precious fragments from the lives of real people magically take us back in time and give us a whirlwind tour of the golden era of Montreal nightlife.

All the images in *Stepping Out* come from the Concordia University Archives.

Stepping Out began as an exhibition at Concordia University's Leonard and Bina Ellen Art Gallery in March 2004. *Montreal Jazz + Clubs* was drawn from the Concordia Archives collection. It accompanied an exhibition of paintings of the period by Montrealer Jack Beder, including some of his paintings of the interiors of Montreal nightclubs.

Stepping Out includes additional archival materials and it expands the time frame of the exhibition. However, it is but a glimpse at a small selection of the hundreds of venues and performers in what was a wild and wonderful period in the history of Montreal.

As an archivist I believe there is value to preserving and examining the past. The past gives us perspective; it helps us know who we were in order to better understand who we are. Our history provides us with context as we reach for the future. The archival materials shown in *Stepping Out* invite us to take a peek into our past as we seek our place in the historical continuum.

For those who knew and loved the clubs, I hope you will be entertained once again by the memories evoked by these snippets from the past. If you've never been to Montreal clubs, I hope you discover a small part of the rich social and cultural history of the wonderful city I call home.

I wasn't around when the clubs, hotels, and theatres were in their glory days, the music swung, and the crowds danced until dawn, so this book is not a personal reminiscence. Neither is it a definitive historical treatment. Rather, *Stepping Out* is an invitation to let some tantalizing images and your own imagination take you back in time.

Nancy Marrelli
Director of Archives
Concordia University

INTRODUCTION

From the 1920s until the early 1950s Montreal had an international reputation as a glamorous wide open city with a lively nightlife.

In this pre-television era people of all ages "stepped out" at night for fun and entertainment. They went to clubs and theatres to socialize, to see their favourite performers and to hear the latest music. In the clubs they might have also enjoyed fancy cocktails or novelty drinks, or maybe had a nice dinner. But mostly people went to clubs to be entertained and to dance the night away. The public was eager to enjoy life in the Flapper or Jazz Era that followed the traumas of World War I. After the stock market Crash in 1929 people were anxious to escape the doldrums of the Great Depression. Everyone looked for diversion from the anxieties of World War II.

Liquor laws in the rest of North America became more and more restricted (Prohibition in the U.S. was in effect 1920-33) but they remained more relaxed in Montreal, except for a brief time at the end of World War I. Clubs, theatres, restaurants, and bars flourished. Montreal's reputation grew as a city of good times and great entertainment. There were hundreds of clubs, lounges, theatres, cafés, and restaurants in which all kinds of entertainment was readily available, and alcohol was legally accessible. There were also many after-hours drinking and gambling spots and prostitution was common despite the pervasive influence and power of the Catholic clergy. Montreal had its own mystique—it was commonly accepted that Montrealers knew how to have a good time! With typical conviviality Montrealers welcomed visitors who came to enjoy the food, the entertainment, and the relaxed liquor laws, and they didn't neglect the more illicit pleasures that were also readily available.

In the vaudeville tradition, many different kinds of entertainment were available in clubs and theatres, offered by both local and touring singers, variety acts, popular and classical musicians, and some amazing novelty acts. The theatres also offered plays and movies. Montreal was an important spot on an entertainment circuit that included North America and some parts of Europe.

The lounges and some of the clubs served drinks only, but many were supper clubs that also had fine dining. In the larger clubs there were often small, cozy bars or lounges available for more intimate socializing. Nightclubs almost always featured dance bands or house bands. Most also had what were called floorshows with featured singers or variety acts, and there was often a chorus line of dancers. Local musicians usually formed the dance bands that played in clubs, theatres and dance halls. In the clubs they also played backup music for the feature performers' acts and they played popular dance music between the shows. Local musicians were only rarely the featured performers. Big-name dance bands were also sometimes brought in as the featured entertainment

The entertainment scene in Montreal and elsewhere included great synergy between the live music scene, radio broadcasting, and the booming recording and sheet music industry. Live radio broadcasts from the clubs promoted the popular bands and the clubs and in turn the recordings and sheet music promoted the clubs, the bands, and the radio broadcasts. Everyone benefited from everyone else's success.

The Montreal club scene was one of complex race, class, and language relations, as well as territorial boundaries. The "downtown" clubs were on St-Antoine Street, where many blacks lived because it was close to the railways where many of the men worked as porters. The "uptown" clubs were in what is now considered downtown Montreal, on or close to Ste-Catherine Street West. The "east-end" clubs were clustered around St. Lawrence (now St-Laurent) Boulevard and Ste-Catherine, Montreal's Red Light District. What was hot and what was not changed frequently. Clubs appeared and disappeared quickly, often in the same locations under different management and with a new name. Bands came together, dissolved and re-formed. Club policy and décor changed frequently as management competed for popularity and market share.

Racial discrimination was prevalent, but it was usually more subtle than in the U.S. There were some notable exceptions. The *Kit Kat Cabaret* on Stanley Street was explicit in its 1932 ads: "Please note that while all the artists in the new revue are colored we welcome white patrons only." There were no segregationist signs at the client entrances to the clubs but there might as well have been for some of

Well-known nightclub chef Nick Morara with Jean Drapeau, possibly at *Club Lido* or *Chez Paree*, 1948[?]
Nick Morara fonds, Concordia University Archives, P192-02-2

them! But black musicians from the U.S. and other parts of Canada were welcome in Montreal and there was an active music scene in the black community, although there was a long history of discrimination in the unions until the early1940s, and mixed black and white bands were not common. At various times it was trendy to have black musicians and black shows, particularly in east-end clubs, but all-white policies were the rule in hotels and were common for uptown clubs in the earlier years. The downtown clubs usually had black musicians and entertainers and their patron policies were wide open. That's where you could almost always find great music, and it was where other musicians went to "jam" after their shows in theatres or clubs in other parts of town.

In the early fifties the entertainment scene changed and the existing complex structure started to crumble, one piece at a time. Commercial television hit the scene in the late 1940s and early 1950s (it came to Montreal in September 1952) and quickly became the entertainment of choice. Audiences dwindled and there was less demand for the acts in the variety shows, so the circuit shrank and withered. Many entertainers left show business, and musicians struggled to earn a living. The broadcasting and record industries were affected and they had to re-invent the way they did business. Added to this serious new threat, in Montreal, lawyer and city official Pacifique (Pax) Plante was a reforming crusader against crime and public corruption. Jean Drapeau was elected mayor of Montreal in October 1954 on a platform to rid the swinging city of vice and corruption. Drapeau aimed a direct hit at the clubs. The freewheeling club scene was largely controlled by the Underworld. Along with the hundreds of clubs operating openly, but sometimes only loosely within the law, after-hours drinking and gambling places and narcotics traffic were also targeted. If all this was not bad enough, when the baby boomers hit adolescence they looked to folk music, rock and roll and other entertainment, and they had little or no interest in floorshows and chorus lines. The clubs declined rapidly; many went out of business, and others reinvented themselves to offer different kinds of entertainment. Entertainers couldn't make a living and many got a day job or left show business. The golden era of *Stepping Out* to glamorous nightclubs faded away in Montreal and elsewhere.

THE RECORDING INDUSTRY IN MONTREAL

Popular American recording artists found a ready market in Montreal from early days. Their appearances in theatres, clubs, and on radio helped bring them to the public eye and boosted local record sales.

Émile Berliner (1851-1929), inventor of the gramophone, moved to Montreal in 1897 after selling his patent in the U.S. The Berliner Company in Montreal made the first commercial recordings in Canada early in the 20th century, and had record stores in the city. It did some original recording and also manufactured for the Canadian market, music recorded elsewhere. These recordings included classical music, opera, choir music, and popular music. Berliner operated under the name Berliner Gramophone between 1904 and 1924. In 1908 the company set up its factory in Montreal's St-Henri district. Émile's older son Herbert founded the independent record pressing company, Compo Company Limited, in the Montreal suburb of Lachine in 1918. In 1921 he feuded with younger brother Edgar who ran Berliner. By 1924 Victor had controlling interests and changed the Berliner name to Victor Talking Machine Company of Canada. In 1929 the Radio Corporation of America (RCA) merged with Victor to create RCA Victor.

Compo operated in Montreal, and from 1921 to 1930 in Toronto. It struggled during the Depression but was able to incorporate Starr-Gannett in the 1930s. Compo did some original recording for their Apex, Sun, Ajax and other labels, including some Montreal musicians such as ragtime pianists Willie Eckstein and his protégée Vera Guilaroff. They also recorded and had the most significant early output of francophone artists for the francophone market in Canada. But a large part of their business was pressing records for Victor, Gannett and other companies for the Canadian market. In 1951 Herbert sold Compo to Decca (for whom Compo had been pressing records in Canada since 1935); Decca was purchased by MCA in 1963. The Lachine factory closed in 1970.

The Musée des ondes Émile Berliner is a modest but growing Montreal museum devoted to the history of sound. It has been open since January 1996 in the former RCA Victor factory complex in St-Henri in Montreal, in the vicinity of the old Berliner factory that was demolished in the 1940s to make way for the new RCA building.

"Lest you Forget", an Apex recording pressed at The
Compo Co., Lachine, Quebec, 1922[?],
Alex Robertson collection, Concordia University Archives,
P023/R0001

"Lest You Forget", sheet music with an image of singer
Joan Zafaro. Montreal, 1922, The Sam Howard Pub. Co.
Alex Robertson collection, Concordia University Archives,
P23-S-489

PROHIBITION

Prohibition in Ontario, the United States, and the Maritime provinces contributed to the growing popularity of Montreal as a good place to come for exciting night life.

Temperance activists operated in Canada through much of the nineteenth century. They advocated Prohibition, making the manufacture, sale, and consumption of alcohol illegal, in varying degrees, to combat the evils of alcoholism. The federal government controlled distilling, import, and export, but the sale of alcohol was a provincial matter so anomalies existed when provinces voted for Prohibition. In March 1918 the federal government made the production, importation, sale, and consumption of alcohol illegal, as part of the War Measures Act. The law was reversed in December 1919 and provincial Prohibition was dropped first in Quebec with others following. Enforcement of Prohibition was difficult and costly; the laws were widely disregarded and they were all eventually repealed, but in some places this took a long time. Prince Edward Island was the last province to drop Prohibition in 1948.

Quebec was the last Canadian province to get Prohibition in 1918 and it was the first to repeal it, in 1919. Temperance never took a strong hold in Quebec as it did in Ontario and the Maritimes.

Prohibition began in the U.S. on January 16, 1920 and it lasted until 1933. During Prohibition in the U.S. there was widespread flagrant violation of the law, including much "rum running" between Canada and the U.S. Except for a very brief period, it was legal in Canada to export alcohol even though it was illegal in the U.S. to import it. Spirits became more popular since they were easier to move around. Speakeasies and illegal drinking and gambling places blossomed in the U.S. The Underworld reaped enormous profits by selling untaxed illegal alcohol and providing illlegal betting and gambling in the speakeasies. Canadian spirits such as Canadian Club whisky, were much in demand but homemade "bathtub gin" was also available. Canada Dry ginger ale became a very popular mixer for less than wonderful home brews during the 1920s, people appreciating the joke as well as the sweet taste that masked the bad taste of the whisky.

Montreal was an attractive destination during Prohibition. Montreal clubs and bars flourished and the city gained a reputation as a great place for a good time. Prohibition added an aspect of "forbidden fruit" to Montreal's "sinful" night life, making it all that much more attractive. The city's "bad" reputation became a tourist asset and attraction. The provincial government raked in the alcohol taxes. Montreal's fabled *joie de vivre* became firmly entrenched and was a source of pride to Montrealers and visitors alike.

Joe Bell scrapbook, Concordia University Archives, B.2p11

RADIO BROADCASTING

The entertainment business worked closely with broadcasters from the very early days of radio. Commercial radio broadcasting began in Canada in 1919 when the first broadcasting licence was issued to Marconi station XWA, Montreal, later to become CFCF. Montreal's CKAC was one of North America's earliest French-language radio station. In the very early years it operated in both English and French with agile bilingual broadcasters such as J. Arthur Dupont and Phil Lalonde.

All things were possible with this exciting new medium and it quickly became clear that programming was needed to fill the airwaves. In an early move towards media concentration newspapers bought or started up radio stations. Montreal's CKAC was owned by *La Presse* until 1969 when it was sold to Télémédia.

Network arrangements were established so local stations could access popular syndicated programming. CKAC was affiliated with the CBS network in 1930 and CFCF developed an affiliation with NBC. Live radio broadcasts from hotel ballrooms and well-known nightclubs were an important part of radio content from 1920 through the 1940s. Broadcasts included popular shows from American networks with which local stations had affiliated, and shows from Montreal clubs. CKAC for example did remotes with the Jack Denny Orchestra from the Mount Royal Hotel's *Normandie Roof*, but by 1930 it was affiliated with the CBS radio network and it also carried Guy Lombardo remotes from the U.S. The airwaves were relatively uncluttered and distant listening was popular, so Montrealers often tuned in to shows from many parts of North America, and local Montreal broadcasts were heard by listeners in many other cities.

CHLP began broadcasting in 1933 from studios in the Sun Life Building in downtown Montreal. It became CFMB in 1962, "a multilingual broadcaster". It took over the former CJMS frequency in 1997.

In 1946 CKVL began operations; it became CNIF in 1999

Pianist and composer Billy Munro at the piano for a CKVL broadcast, 1946[?]
Jack Tietolman fonds, Concordia University Archives, P113-02-158

The Golden Age
of Montreal Night Clubs
1925 - 1955

The Melody Kings

The Melody Kings were a popular Montreal "hot dance" band in the 1920s. They were a fixture at the *Jardin de Danse* when it was on Bleury below Ste-Catherine, and they played long engagements at the *Palace Theatre* on Ste-Catherine Street, and later at the toney *Ritz-Carlton Hotel*, from where they were broadcast live on radio. They played at many of the dozens of other clubs and dance halls that were popular around Montreal in the 1920s. The music was hot and so was the band! American banjo player Andy Tipaldi (1894-1969) put the band together. It included pianist Billy Munro, who had an earlier dance band at the *Jardin de Danse*. Munro wrote the music for "When My Baby Smiles at Me" and he also co-wrote (with Willy Eckstein) "Music(Makes the World Go 'Round)". Munro was a long--time favourite in Montreal. In 1930, after a hiatus and the 1929 stock market Crash, the Melody Kings played at the *Beaux Arts*, a club on Stanley Street owned at the time by Andy Tipaldi; it would later become the location of *Club Lido* and finally, the *Chez Paree*, which is still there, though it has long been a strip club and is now also a casino. The Melody Kings made a number of recordings with the Berliner company in Montreal. The photo of the popular Melody Kings on the sheet music would certainly have helped sales in Montreal.

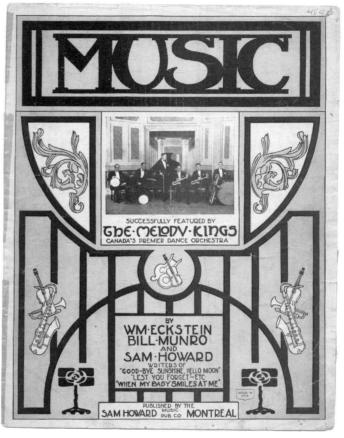

"The Midnight Waltz", sheet music with an image of the Melody Kings in Montreal. Toronto, 1925, Leo Feist Limited
John Gilmore fonds, Concordia University Archives, P004

"Music (Makes the World Go 'Round)", sheet music with an image of the Melody Kings in Montreal. Montreal, 1923, Sam Howard Music Pub Co.
Alex Robertson collection, Concordia University Archives, P023-S-0484

Vera Guilaroff

Vera Guilaroff (1902-76) grew up in Montreal and began her career as an accompanist for silent films at Montreal's *Regent Theatre*. The *Regent Theatre* opened in 1916 at Park Avenue and Laurier. Guilaroff frequently performed popular novelty rag music on radio and in theatres and nightclubs from the 1920s to the 1940s, in Canada, the U.S.A., and Britain. In later years she composed. She was a protégée of legendary Montreal piano player Willie Eckstein with whom she frequently worked. She performed for the first remote broadcast of Montreal's XWA (later CFCF) Radio in 1923, and she made seven recordings with Compo in Montreal in the 1920s. She was sometimes called "The Princess of the Radio".

Autographed photograph of piano player Vera Guilaroff, 1925[?]
John Gilmore fonds/courtesy Jim Kidd, Concordia University Archives, P004-02-146

Inscription reads: To my very dear friend Jim Kidd, Fondly, Vera Guilaroff

Willie Eckstein

Willie Eckstein was a teenage vaudeville star who was billed as "The Boy Paderewski". The diminutive "Mr. Fingers" had classical training in piano and played in the "novelty rag" style. He was a composer of ragtime and popular songs, including patriotic songs that supported the war effort. In Montreal he earned a reputation as a gifted live accompanist to silent movies, particularly at Montreal's *Strand Theatre*. *The Strand* was one of the first important movie houses in Montreal, and Willie Eckstein will forever be linked with the theatre. It was built in 1912 on Ste-Catherine at Mansfield. (It was demolished in 1973.)

In 1919 Willie Eckstein performed for one of the first live radio performances in North America at radio station XWA (later known as CFCF). He also played at *Wood Hall*, and the opening of both the *Corona* (1923) and *Snowdon* (1937) Theatres. Willie often collaborated with his protégée Vera Guilaroff. After 1930 Willie Eckstein concentrated on radio and cabaret appearances, playing at many clubs, theatres, and halls all over Montreal and the surrounding area, including the *Piccadilly*, the *Carioca*, and the *Savoy*. He did long stints at the *Château Ste-Rose*, and in later years the *Clover Café* and the *Berkeley Hotel*. He died soon after being honoured at the closing of *Her Majesty's Theatre* on Guy Street in May 1963.

Her/His Majesty's Theatre opened in 1899 on Guy Street. It was variously called Her Majesty's (after Queen Victoria), Proctor's Theatre, His Majesty's, and then again Her Majesty's (with the coronation of Elizabeth II). It was a landmark Montreal venue for live theatre, both classical and popular music performances (including home to the MSO for a decade), as well as a movie theatre. The theatre was next to the Corona Hotel and later the Corona Tavern; the Stork Club opened next door in the late 1930s and it was popular with theatre goers at intermission or after the show. Her Majesty's went into decline and it was totally eclipsed by the 1963 opening of Place des Arts. It closed and was demolished in May 1963. The grand chandelier from Her Majesty's can still be seen in all its glory on the main floor of Ogilvy's Department Store.

"Lonesome Rose", sheet music with an image of Elsie Thevernard. Montreal, 1923, Sam Howard Music Publishing Company
Alex Robertson collection, Concordia University Archives, P023-S-00412

"The Lost Melody", sheet music with a silhouette of composer Willy Eckstein. Montreal 1932. Elldee Publishing Company
Alex Robertson collection, Concordia University Archives, P023-S-00483

Records Pressed in Montreal

Recording companies did well in Montreal in the early years of the 20th century. They did a limited number of original recordings, but they also pressed records for the Canadian market for major American record labels. By 1924 Victor were majority owners of Berliner, Canada's first record-pressing company, and by1929 Victor became RCA Victor. Compo's Lachine factory manufactured for Decca from 1935, and Decca bought Compo in 1951. Touring recording artists helped increase the sales of records. These popular recording artists brought in large crowds when they played in the local clubs.

"Strolling on the Mountain", a private 78 rpm recording pressed at RCA Victor Company Limited, Montreal, 1920s[?]
Lyrics and music by Willie Eckstein, piano Willie Eckstein, and vocalist R. Brault
Alex Robertson collection, Concordia University Archives, P023-R-0018

"Blueberry Hill", a Decca 78 rpm recording pressed at The Compo Co. Limited, Lachine, Quebec, date unknown, 1940s[?]
Lyrics and music by Al Lewis, Larry Stock, Vincent Rose, Gordon Jenkins and His Orchestra
Alex Robertson Collection, Concordia University Archives, P023-R-0070

Connie's Inn

Connie's Inn was at 1417 St. Lawrence (now St-Laurent) Boulevard near Ste-Catherine. This was the same spot where the earlier *Frolics Cabaret* had featured headliner American performers. The new club took the same name as a club in Harlem at 131st and 7th Avenue that was famous even outside New York City as a showcase for talented black performers playing to white audiences. Many other Montreal clubs used the names of famous nightclubs in New York, London, or Paris.

Advertising brochure for the opening of *Connie's Inn* (formerly the *Frolics*), Saturday, May 20, 1933
Myron Sutton scrapbook, Concordia University Archives, S.1p4

Connie's Inn

Montreal became well known as a wide-open city in the American Prohibition era (1920-33) and the nightclub scene was hot, even during the Depression. The opening of Montreal's *Connie's Inn* featured black performers from New York as well as a Canadian swing band that had recently arrived from Ontario, the Canadian Ambassadors, led by Myron Sutton. The *Montmartre* relocated to this spot in the 1950s from around the corner on Ste-Catherine.

Advertising flyer for *Connie's Inn*
Myron Sutton scrapbook, Concordia University Archives, S.1p6c

Invitation to the June 15, 1933 official opening of *Connie's Inn*
Myron Sutton scrapbook, Concordia University Archives, S.1p7b

Chez Maurice 1933

Phil Maurice opened *Chez Maurice* on St-Alexandre near Ste-Catherine in 1931. The club would have many incarnations. In 1932 *Chez Maurice* moved to an upstairs location at 1244 Ste-Catherine Street, near Mountain (now de la Montagne) where the *Venetian Gardens* had opened in 1919. This site would house a succession of *Chez Maurice* clubs. In 1933 *Chez Maurice* was a popular upscale café-cabaret offering dinner, dancing, and a floorshow. Radio broadcasts of dance music were done from the club in the 1930s. Phil Maurice moved on at the end of the 1930s to become impresario at the prestigious *His Majesty's Theatre*.

Advertising flyer for *Chez Maurice*, 1933 summer season
Joe Bell scrapbook, Concordia University Archives, B.2p10

Chez Maurice 1937

Patrons came to *Chez Maurice* to dine and to see top acts such as torch singer Helen Morgan; the All-Coloured Review starring Billie Holiday (1942); the Mills Brothers (1942); and Mel Tormé (1949). But the crowds especially came to dance. In the 1930s they danced to the tunes of local bands led by Charles Kramer, Alex Lajoie, and Jimmy Laing. In the early 1940s the enterprising Roland David led the house band, but *Chez Maurice Danceland* also brought in idolized American headliner swing bands. *Chez Maurice* constantly re-invented itself and the crowds kept coming. After the last *Chez Maurice* closed its doors, the second-floor space had various tenants, including the Canadian Broadcasting Corporation briefly in the 1950s; it was vacant for some time, and is currently the upper floor of the retail store Urban Outfitters.

You

are cordially invited to attend the

grand re-opening of the

CHEZ MAURICE

CANADA'S FINEST CAFE

MONDAY

MARCH EIGHT

NINETEEN HUNDRED AND THIRTY-SEVEN

•

In Conjunction with this Event We
Offer for Your Approval, Montreal's
Newest and Smartest Rendezvous

CLUB DEAUVILLE

NEVER A COVER CHARGE

DINNER DE LUXE

Served from 6 to 10 p.m.

★

Presenting

"CHEZ MAURICE PARADE OF 1937"

Salute a Stunning New Musical Joy Ride
with all the Smartness and Variety and
Zest Chez Maurice are Famed for!
A Grand All-around Show

featuring

DEONE PARISH

in Songs Delightfully Indiscreet

•

Added Attraction!

Incomparable Continuous Dance Music
from 7 p.m. to Closing

CHARLES KRAMER

and His Orchestra

(Limited Engagement)

and

ALEX LAJOIE

and His Chez Maurice Orchestra

•

3 SHOWS NIGHTLY

1244 St. Catherine St. W.   Reservations - MA. 4114

An invitation to the March 1937 re-opening of *Chez Maurice*
Joe Bell scrapbook, Concordia University Archives, B.2p13b

Club Deauville at Chez Maurice

Club Deauville was a new cocktail bar at *Chez Maurice* when the club re-opened in the spring of 1937. The *Deauville* was a more intimate space than the large club space which offered dining, dancing, and a floorshow. The *Deauville* menu offers a large selection of cocktails, fizzes, sours, mixed drinks, and cordials that were popular in the 1930s.

Musician Joe Bell (1908-72) played in the 1930s and 1940s with the Charles Kramer Orchestra that was frequently featured at *Chez Maurice*, the nearby *Club Lido*, and the *Normandie Roof*, as well as other Montreal clubs. From 1945 to 1965 Bell played trombone with the Montreal Symphony Orchestra and taught music at McGill University. During his career as a jazz musician Joe Bell kept a scrapbook of Montreal nightclub memorabilia and clippings. The Bell family deposited Joe's treasured scrapbook in the Concordia University Archives in 1987.

Front and back of menu, *Club Deauville* at *Chez Maurice*, 1937[?]
Joe Bell scrapbook, Concordia University Archives, B.2p23

CLUB DEAUVILLE

COCKTAILS

Locker No.		Service
98	Ward 8	.55
99	Rhum	.50
100	Old Fashioned	.50
101	Manhattan	.45
102	Dry Martini	.35
103	Orange Blossom	.50
104	Bronx	.45
105	Dubonnet	.35
106	Alexander	.55
107	Pink Lady	.50
108	Bacardi or Daquiri	.65
109	Side Car	.55
110	White Lady	.55
111	Clover Club	.50
112	Perfect	.45
113	Rob. Roy	.45
114	Stinger	.60
115	Cup o' Cheer	.55
116	Coffee	.60
117	Champagne	1.00
118	Gimlet	.60
119	Rhum Cola	.60

FLIPS

120	Sherry Flip	.60
121	Brandy Flip	.60
122	Gin Flip	.50
123	Brandy Egg Nog	.75

FIZZES

Locker No.		Service
124	Silver Fizz	.60
125	Golden Fizz	.60
126	Royal Fizz	.60
127	Imperial Fizz	.60
128	Sloe Gin Fizz	.60

SOURS

129	Brandy	.55
130	Gin	.55
131	Whiskey	.55
132	Rye	.55
133	Rhum	.55
134	Sloe Gin	.55

MIXED DRINKS

136	Rhum Swizzle	.60
137	Cuba Liba	.75
138	Gin Daisy	.60
139	Pink Lady	.55
140	Amer Picon	.75
141	Horses Neck (Plain or Rye)	.55 and .70
142	White Cap	.45

COLLINS and RICKEYS

143	John Collins	.50
144	Gin Rickey	.50
145	Sloe Gin Rickey	.60
146	Gin Buck	.60
147	Mamie Taylor	.60

Beers and Ales 30c per Bottle

COBBLERS

Locker No.		Service
148	Whiskey	.55
149	Brandy	.55
150	Sherry	.55
151	Port	.55

WHISKIES

152	Scotch Domestic	.45
153	Scotch Imported	.50
	Special Brands Dewars Ne Plus Ultra, etc.	.60

GIN

154	Canadian	.40
155	Imported	.45 and .55
156	Sloe Gin	.50

BRANDIES

157	Monet V.V.S.O.P. 40 yr. old	.65
158	Hennessy ★★★	.60
159	Martell	.60
160	Monet	.50

RYE

161	Domestic Rye	.40
162	Seagrams V.O.	.50
	Candian Club	.50

RHUM

Locker No.		Service
163	Demarara	.40
164	Jamaica	.40
165	Bacardi Superior	.60
176	St. James	.60

CORDIALS and LIQUEURS

166	Chartreuse Green	.50
168	Benedictine	.45
169	Cointreau	.45
170	Creme de Menthe	.40
171	Kummel	.50
172	Cherry Brandy	.45
173	Creme de Cocoa	.45
174	Grand Marnier	.50
175	Brandy Inhaler	.75
177	Apricot Brandy	.45
178	Peach Brandy	.45
179	Maraschino	.50
180	Blackberry Brandy	.45
181	Curacao	.45
182	Pousse Cafe	.75

PUNCHES

183	Planters	.60
184	Brandy	.60
185	Rhum	.60

MONTREAL'S ULTRA - SMART RENDEZVOUS

Inside menu, *Club Deauville* at *Chez Maurice*, ca 1937
Joe Bell scrapbook, Concordia University Archives, B.2p23

Ina Ray Hutton and Her Melodears

Ina Ray Hutton and Her Melodears appeared in Montreal in 1936, playing at the *Loews Theatre* on November 7. On November 10 they played at *Chez Maurice* and did a live radio broadcast. This band was typical of the kind of act that appeared in Montreal theatres and clubs and on the radio in the 1930s and 1940s. Ina Ray Hutton (1916-84) was the only prominent female bandleader of the era. She began her career as a dancer, and part of her popularity was due to her rather seductive dancing on stage while conducting her band. The Melodears lasted from 1934-39 and she had another all-female band between 1950 and 1956. In 1940 she formed an all-male band, Ina Ray Hutton and Her Great All-New Male Orchestra, and in December 1943 they played at the *Auditorium*. This was a popular licensed dancehall at 375 Ontario West (now President Kennedy), near Bleury. The *Bellevue Casino* would open on the same site in the late 1940s.

Publicity photograph of Ina Ray Hutton and Her Melodears, 1936[?] Photo: Mills Artists, Inc. N.Y.
Joe Bell scrapbook, Concordia University Archives, B.1p3

Exotic Dancer Rosita Royce

Rosita Royce was an exotic dancer well known to Montreal audiences in the 1930s and 1940s. She used trained birds in her act, the birds perching and flying around her. She was a headline attraction at the 1936 California Pacific Exposition in San Diego where she reputedly stripped completely except for the birds. Performers worked hard to develop distinctive acts, and many had a faithful following. This photo is in the Joe Bell scrapbook and it is possible that Rosita Royce appeared in a Montreal club like *Chez Maurice* when Bell played there in the house band. Rosita was also a frequent performer at the old *Gayety Theatre*.

Strippers like Sally Rand and Lili St. Cyr performed regularly in Montreal theatres and clubs. Performers' publicity photos were used as calling cards and they usually clearly identified the performer and the act. They were given to local media by both the artist and the club in which the artist was appearing, to drum up as much publicity as possible, but entertainers also exchanged them.

Autographed publicity photograph of exotic dancer Rosita Royce, 1937[?]
Photo: Bruno of Hollywood NYC
Joe Bell scrapbook, Concordia University Archives, B.1p47

Dedication reads: To Joe – Thanks for the re-write job – I wish you lots of success
– Rosita Royce and "Silly Billy" (white cockatoo) and "Red" (macaw)

Cab Calloway at Chez Maurice 1943

The *Chez Maurice* nightclub in the heart of downtown Montreal became *Chez Maurice Danceland* in the 1940s. It no longer served dinner or featured a floorshow. As the war progressed it came to be seen as unseemly that Montreal was enjoying itself so much and the number of clubs selling alcohol was reduced. *Chez Maurice* became one of the officially unlicensed Montreal dance clubs where teenagers could dance to popular big-name American bands led by Cab Calloway, Jimmy Dorsey, Duke Ellington, Jimmy Lunceford and others. Patrons often came equipped with their own liquor in hip flasks.

Dinty Moore's Restaurant, a popular spot that was famous for corned beef and cabbage, was conveniently located downstairs from the second-floor club. Dinty Moore's was named after the restaurant in the comic strip "Bringing Up Father" that ran from 1913-2000. It featured the human foibles of an Irish-American couple called Maggie and Jiggs, who had humble beginnings but came into unexpected money. The snobbish Maggie and daughter Nora were constantly at odds with the down-to-earth Jiggs whose favourite entertainment was a corned beef and cabbage dinner at the downscale Dinty Moore's Restaurant and an evening out with his old neighbourhood pals. "Bringing Up Father" was a popular comic strip in the difficult days of the 1930s and 1940s.

The crowd in this photo is mixed black and white, but this was not always the case in the uptown clubs.

Cab Calloway and his Cotton Club Orchestra playing to a young audience
at *Chez Maurice*, November 29, 1943
John Gilmore fonds, Concordia University Archives, P004-02-05

The Canadian Ambassadors at the Hollywood Club

The Canadian Ambassadors under the direction of Myron "Mynie" Sutton, played in Guelph, Ontario and Aylmer, Quebec in 1931-32. They moved to Montreal in 1933 to become the city's first significant black Canadian jazz band. The Ambassadors were active until 1939, although they changed size and composition many times. They had an enviable record of employment for any band during the early 1930s, despite the Depression. When Montreal's *Connie's Inn* opened in May 1933 the Canadian Ambassadors were billed as "The Colored Kings of Jazz." They remained at *Connie's Inn* for nearly a year and later played a long stint at the *Hollywood Club*. They later played to packed houses at the *Montmartre* for a year and also did radio broadcasts. They were extremely popular in these east-end clubs.

The Canadian Ambassadors, *Hollywood Club*, 1934[?] Photo: Acme Studio
Myron Sutton fonds, Concordia University Archives, P019-02-57

From left: Andy Shorter, Benny Starks, Myron Sutton, Terry Hooper, feature vocalist
Evelyn Campbell, Ernie Baker, Clyde Duncan, Lloyd Duncan, Brad Moxley.

Toots Henderson

Toots Henderson was a specialty dancer from New York. Her publicity photo beautifully illustrates the type of costume worn by Harlem dancers who were featured performers at Montreal clubs and theatres in the 1920s and 1930s.

The photograph is part of the extensive scrapbook Mynie Sutton created documenting his musical career, especially in Montreal. The Sutton family donated the scrapbook to the Concordia University Archives in 1984.

Toots Henderson appeared at the *Gayety Theatre*, located very close to the east-end clubs where Mynie Sutton played with the Canadian Ambassadors. She may have appeared in a Montreal club or theatre at the same time Mynie's Canadian Ambassadors were booked there or in a nearby club.

Autographed publicity photo of Toots Henderson, 1934[?] Photo: Woodard's Studio N.Y.C.
Myron Sutton scrapbook, Concordia University Archives, 1.p22a

The inscriptions reads: To the sweetist (sic) man in Montreal — From a dear friend,
Tit Henderson

"War" – a special cabaret evening at the Stadium Ballroom

Mynie Sutton's Canadian Ambassadors and the complete *Club Hollywood* floorshow were features in this special Sunday evening cabaret at the *Stadium Ballroom*. This dance hall was at De Lorimier and Ontario, near the De Lorimier Stadium (home to baseball's Montreal Royals, where Jackie Robinson would make history in 1946). The evening featured 30 competing performers, and "One hour of fast Red Hot Dancing, Singing and Entertainment". The Ambassadors had moved from *Connie's Inn* to *Club Hollywood* in March 1934.

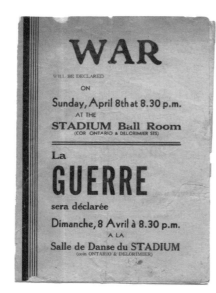 

Cover and back cover of promotional brochure for "War",
a special cabaret evening at the *Stadium Ballroom*, Sunday, April 8, 1934
Myron Sutton scrapbook, Concordia University Archives, S.2p29a

At the 1st Annual Festival of Music

BETWEEN

7 FAMOUS DANCE ORCHESTRAS 7

FEATURING

GEO. SIMS and his Orchestra
KEN LARGE and his Orchestra
HENRY ALBERT and his Rhythm Kings
HAL CLARK and his Broadway Collegians
MYRON SUTTON and his Can. Ambassadors
Colored Rythm and Hot Syncopation

Also 2 others famous colored and white Orchestras.

20 ACTS OF STAR CABARET FEATURES 20

Come and cheer for your favorite Orchestra at this

GIGANTIC WAR OF JAZZ

The Greatest Dance of the Season.

DON'T MISS THIS NIGHT. CONTINUOUS DANCING, ENTERTAINMENT, REVELRY. COME AND BRING YOUR FRIENDS.

Don't forget the date: Sunday APRIL 8th, at 8.30 p.m.

Organizers: Paul LAPORTE, Gérard DEMEULE, Nick BIOCCA

Admission: 50c. Plus Tax   Checking: 10c.

Under the Personal Direction of TED MARKS

Au 1er Festival de Musique Annuel

ENTRE

7 FAMEUX ORCHESTRES DE DANSE 7

COMPRENANT

GEO. SIMMS et son Orchestre
KEN LARGE et son Orchestre
HENRY ALBERT et ses Rhythm Kings
HAL CLARK et ses Broadway Collegians
MYRON SUTTON et ses Can. Ambassadors
Fameux Orchestre de Couleur au Canada

En plus 2 autres Orchestres bien connus.

20 NUMEROS DE VAUDEVILLE DE PREMIERE CLASSE 20

Venez et choisissez votre Orchestre favorite à cette

GRANDE BATAILLE D'ORCHESTRE

Le plus grand évènement de la Saison.

UNE SOIREE DE PLAISIR INOUBLIABLE.   VENEZ VOUS AMUSEZ.
AMENEZ VOS AMIS.

N'oubliez pas la date: Dimanche 8 AVRIL à 8.30 p.m.

Organisateurs: Paul LAPORTE, Gérard DEMEULE, Nick BIOCCA

Admission: 50c. Plus Taxe   Vestiaire: 10c.

Direction Personnel de TED MARKS

Inside spread of promotional brochure for "War",
a special cabaret evening at the *Stadium Ballroom*, Sunday, April 8, 1934
Myron Sutton scrapbook, Concordia University Archives, S.2p29a

Club Hollywood

The *Club Hollywood* was at 92 Ste-Catherine East, near St. Lawrence, and within short walking distance of several other east-end clubs: *Connie's Inn* (where the *Frolics* was located earlier), the *Montmartre*, *Blue Sky*, and the *Chinese Paradise Grill*. Until the late 1930s (and again later) these east-end clubs mostly featured black entertainers playing for a white audience. The Canadian Ambassadors played at the *Hollywood* March 1934-June 1935, also doing live radio broadcasts from there. The club offered dining, dancing, and a floorshow. Entertainers had the same unusual working hours and they often socialized together; the members of the Canadian Ambassadors belonged to *Club Hollywood's* amateur baseball team.

In the 1920s there was a *Hollywood Club* in New York City, at Broadway and 49th Street, Times Square.

A GALA OPENING SAT. NOV. 10th

WITH AN

ALL STAR CAST

FEATURING

"BOB WILLIAMS M. C."

Visit us and enjoy the hot rythm dance melodies

of

"MYRON SUTTON'S AMBASSADORS"

Canada's Only Colored Broadcasting Dance Orchestra.

92 St. Catherine East

Dear Member,

It is with pride that we announce the engagement of this new show and in thanking you for your patronage of the past year, invite you to avail yourself of the excellent cuisine, intimate atmosphere, fine dancing and courteous service of your own

CLUB HOLLYWOOD

Very truly yours,

PERCY L. MUSTART,

Manager

Phones:
HA. 1861
PL. 0412

Be sure and make your reservation early.

CALL

HArbour 1861 :-: PLateau 0412

VISIT THE

HOLLYWOOD CLUB

Announcement Extraordinary

Promotional handout for *Club Hollywood*, front, back & interior, November 1934
Myron Sutton scrapbook, Concordia University Archives S.1p20b

Chinese Paradise

The *Chinese Paradise* was a popular club in Montreal's Chinatown; it was sometimes called the *Chinese Paradise Grill*. It was owned and operated by the Wong family. The club maintained a black entertainer policy until the spring of 1938 when many east-end clubs started switching to white acts.

Press clipping,
date and source unknown
Myron Sutton scrapbook, Concordia
University Archives, S.1p36e

Dancer (probably Lola Milroy) with Myron Sutton and the Canadian Ambassadors on stage at the *Chinese Paradise*, 1935[?]
Myron Sutton scrapbook, Concordia University Archives, S.1p36e

Dedication reads: To Mynie a fellow I am glad I know,
here's wishing you what I wish myself Freddye

Herb Johnson at the Chinese Paradise

Connecticut-born Herb Johnson had a Quebec connection. His mother was a francophone born in St-Hyacinthe. When he arrived in Montreal the first band he put together played at the *Chinese Paradise* at 57 de la Gauchetière West.

Herb Johnson Band at the *Chinese Paradise* club, 1936[?]
Herb Johnson fonds, Concordia University Archives, P088-02-20

From left: Arthur Davis, Vernon Blackman, Herb Johnson, Augustus Johnson,
"Cornet" Browne. Herb Johnson's Dewey saxophone sits on the stand

The Montmartre

The *Montmartre* opened at 59 Ste-Catherine Street, just west of St. Lawrence (now St-Laurent) Boulevard on September 29, 1937. It was a typical Montreal east-end club originally with black entertainers and a predominantly white audience. Myron Sutton's Canadian Ambassadors were the featured house band for nearly a year, as *Montmartre* became one of the hot nightspots in Montreal's legendary wide-open club scene. In the 1950s the *Montmartre* moved around the corner to 1417 St. Lawrence, the location where the *Frolics Cabaret* had ushered in Montreal's Golden Age of Nightclubs, and where *Connie's Inn* had drawn night-clubbers to the heart of the Red Light District. In 1972 the Ste-Catherine Street location became the home of Véhicule Art (Montréal) Inc. (1972-82), Montreal's first artist-run gallery space. Véhicule stayed in this space until the summer of 1979, and gallery members were sometimes told by oldtimers that the space had been a blind pig, or illegal after-hours drinking and gambling club in earlier days.

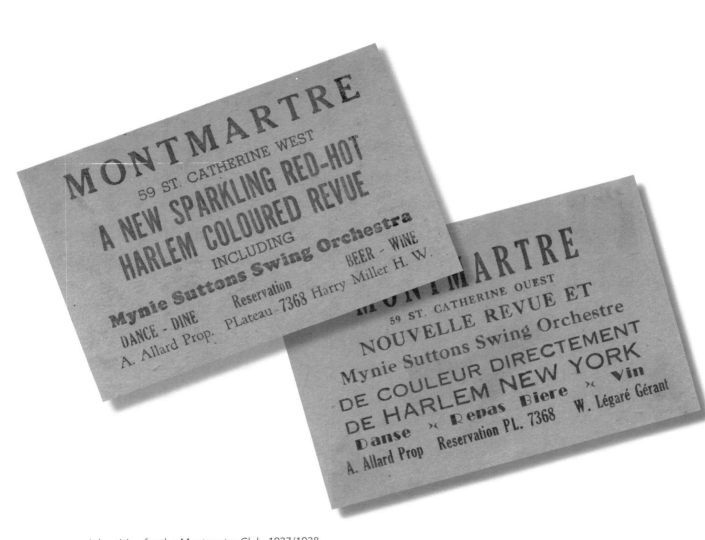

Advertising for the *Montmartre Club*, 1937/1938
Myron Sutton scrapbook, Concordia University Archives, S.2p10a

Fan letter to Mynie Sutton
from a radio listener 1937

Live-on-location radio broadcasts of dance bands and variety shows in nightclubs, hotels, and theatres were a significant feature of the North American entertainment scene from the early days of commercial radio in the 1920s through the 1940s. Local stations often had connections to larger networks where big-name bands broadcast out of well-known clubs or hotel ballrooms. This was an inexpensive and appealing entertainment, especially during the Depression. Radio broadcasts traveled far and wide so these shows reached a large audience and helped popularize the music, the entertainers, and the venues from which they were broadcast. The music and glamorous café society lifestyle were further reinforced by popular movies. The Canadian Ambassadors broadcast dance music regularly from the *Montmartre*, and there were many other broadcasts from other Montreal clubs and theatres as well.

Translation of the letter:

Montreal, November 8, 1937

Dear Sir,
I am eager to write to sincerely thank you for having played specially for me and for Denise, the lovely piece, B and T[?] with your lively orchestra.

I eagerly listen to all the radio broadcasts from the "Montmartre Cabaret" and I hope that all the listeners will have the pleasure of hearing you on the radio for a long time.

With my sincere thanks, I remain
Pauline St Amand

Montréal, le 8 Novembre 1937

Cher Monsieur,

Je m'empresse de vous écrire pour vous remercier très sincèrement d'avoir bien voulu jouer tout spéciale- ment à mon intention ain- si qu'à Denise, votre belle fantaisie B. and T. avec votre extraordinaire orchestre.

J'écoute avec un vif intérêt la radiodiffusion de

tous les programmes du "Cabaret Montmartre" et j'espère que tous les radio- philes auront encore la joie de vous entendre très longtemps à la radio.

Veuillez recevoir mes plus sincères remerciements.

Votre très obligée

Pauline St Amand.

Fan letter to Mynie Sutton from a radio listener, November 8, 1937
Myron Sutton scrapbook, Concordia University, S.2.p2de

Club Montmartre

Dancers in costume and other club staff pose with bandleader Myron "Mynie" Sutton (centre) and his *Canadian Ambassadors*. Note the unusual backdrop and the boxing gloves and images of popular hero, boxer Joe Louis. The "Brown Bomber" had won the Heavyweight Boxing Championship a few months earlier in June of 1937. In 1938 the *Montmartre* management switched to white shows, and other east-end clubs soon adopted the same policy. The *Canadian Ambassadors* began a decline as their usual engagements had simply disappeared and the venues where they could play were very limited. The Depression was in full swing and Sutton and the band struggled to make a living. In 1941 Sutton left Montreal for his native Niagara Falls where he got a day job, settled down and had a family. Sutton led bands and played music part-time there until his death in 1982.

The Canadian Ambassadors, dancers, and other *Club Montmartre* personnel, October 6, 1937 Photo: Roger Janelle. Myron Sutton fonds, Concordia University Archives, P019-02-08

Back row, from left: Club owner Adolphe Alard and musicians Willy Wade, Harold "Steep" Wade, Myron Sutton, Benny Montgomery, Bill Kersey, Brad Moxley

The Terminal Club

The *Terminal Club* was in the heart of Montreal's black community. It opened in the 1920s across from the CPR's Windsor train station. It was an unassuming gathering place for black musicians and it became an after-hours spot where musicians could jam and clients could continue to party after the uptown clubs closed. The *Terminal Club* was an important venue for black entertainers—Mynie Sutton led the small house band there in the late 1930s as work became increasingly scarce for black bands.

Mae Johnson Stars At Terminal Club

Replacing Babe Wallace, who has joined Ella Fitzgerald's orchestra in capacity as Maestro, is the swingsational cotton club star Mae Johnson, whose magnetic personality and outstanding talent has been the talk of the Great White Way in New York. No less a versatile entertainer is Mae Diggs making her initial appearance in Montreal.

Then there is the exotic Lucille O'Daniel rendering her conception of an Oriental fantasy and Sara Cheek gives out with a novelty song "You, You, You." Bubbles and Millie swing out a terrific dance routine and Ed. Perkins dispenses dance-inducing music. Grace Allen rounds out the floor-show in steliar fashion.

Swing is King—True Harlemese Atmosphere

The TERMINAL

Presents

"HARLEM on PARADE"

A Star-Studded Sepia Revue

Plus

Mynie Suttons' Swingsters

Southern Fried Chicken — Our Specialty

St. Antoine and Windsor   MArquette 0500

Terminal Club publicity (1940) and ad (1937), *Montreal Standard*
Meilan Lam fonds, Concordia University, P135

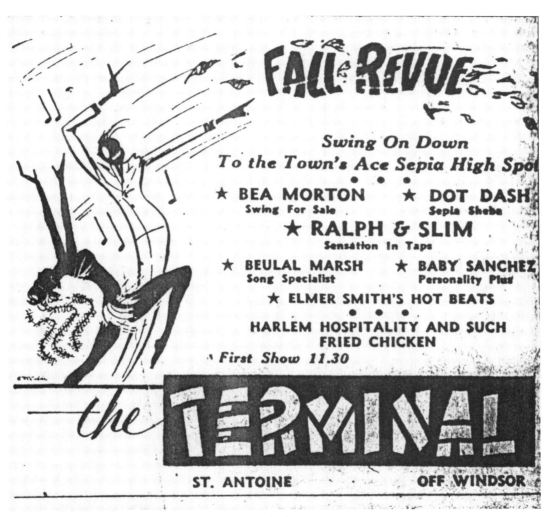

The *Terminal Club* ad (1937) *Montreal Standard*
Meilan Lam fonds, Concordia University Archives, P135

Herb Johnson at the Roseland Ballroom

The *Roseland Ballroom* opened in March 1921 on Phillips Square (Ste-Catherine near Aylmer), but it later moved to Ontario (now President Kennedy) near Bleury, the location that would become the *Auditorium* and later the *Bellevue Casino*. Bands formed and dissolved to meet the needs of the moment, but this version of the Herb Johnson band at *Roseland* included Hugh Sealey, Will "Mack" Mackenzie, Elmer Smith, Freddy Blackburn, and Clyde Duncan. The *Roseland Ballroom* in Montreal took its name from the famous New York City nightspot that opened in Times Square (52nd and Broadway) in 1919, originally for whites only. The legendary New York club has had its ups and downs, but the large space (over 3,000 standing capacity) is still in use for concerts, fashion shows, special events and award shows. Montreal's *Roseland* is long gone.

Herb Johnson and his Roseland Orchestra, 1938[?] Photo: La Photo Modèle
John Gilmore fonds, courtesy Herb Johnson, Concordia University Archives, P-004-02-97

Herb Johnson at Café St. Michel

Herb Johnson first came to Montreal in 1935, during the hard times of the Depression, and he ended up making the area home for the rest of his life. In the 1930s and 1940s he worked in many clubs, including the *Chinese Paradise*, the *Washington Club*, the *Roseland Ballroom*, and the *Gayety Theatre*. In the 1940s he joined Louis Metcalfe's International Band at *Café St. Michel*. Johnson did the arrangements of popular songs in the cutting edge be-bop style that the Metcalfe band introduced to Canada. Johnson was a respected musician, teacher, and arranger who became a mainstay of the Montreal music scene. He played in the Montreal area for more than five decades, with his own band at the *Belmar* and the *Savoy*, with many other bands, and as a sideman in virtually all the local clubs, lounges, and theatres. He played well into his eighties with the Senior Musicians Orchestra which he organized and led. Herb Johnson and his son Coleman donated Johnson's archives to the Concordia Archives in 1993.

Herb Johnson playing a solo with Louis Metcalf's International Band, *Café St. Michel*, April 1947
Photo: Louis Jacques, Canada Wide Feature Service Ltd.
Herb Johnson fonds, Concordia University Archives, P088-02-01

The Normandie Roof, atop the Mount Royal Hotel

The *Normandie Roof* was a posh club at the top of the prestigious *Sheraton Mount Royal Hotel*, for which it was a prime attraction. This stylishly appointed supper club featured sophisticated dining, dancing, and entertainment aimed at white audiences. Radio station CKAC's Phil Lalonde hosted English and French Saturday night remote broadcasts of the Jack Denny Band from the *Normandie Roof* in the 1920s. Live broadcasts were frequently done by other stations and from other clubs. These broadcasts were beneficial to the broadcaster, the club, and the musicians during this golden age of radio, the big band, and Montreal nightclubs. The CFCF radio studios were located in the penthouse of the Mount Royal Hotel between 1927 and 1935.

Maître d'hôtel Victor Prévost of the *Normandie Roof*, as he appears with patrons in a *Montreal Standard* spread on Montreal nightlife, April 28, 1951
Nick Morara fonds, Concordia University Archives, P195

The *Normandie Roof* Cigarette Girl, Lorraine Crane, as she appears in a *Montreal Standard* spread on Montreal nightlife, April 28, 1951
Nick Morara fonds, Concordia University Archives, P195

Thrill in the carefree, comfortable, sophisticated atmosphere of
"America's Most Beautiful Room"

The NORMANDIE ROOF

atop the Mount Royal Hotel, where the temperature is always 70 degrees cool.

The *Normandie Roof*, atop the *Mount Royal Hotel*, 1937. Inside front cover of "Current Events",
the official organ of the Province of Quebec Hotel Ass'n. Inc., August 20, 1937
Joe Bell scrapbook, Concordia University Archives, 2.p3a

Club Lido, 1931

Club Lido opened in Montreal in the early 1930s. It was named for the legendary *Lido* in Paris. From the late 19th century, nightclubs with revues or floorshows were part of glamorous Paris nightlife. The original *Lido* in Paris was established on the Champs-Elysées in the era known as the Belle Époque. It was a lavish nightclub named for the long, narrow island that separates Venice from the Adriatic. The Paris *Lido* was a legend by the 1920s, with elaborate shows and décor that had been inspired by the beach on Venice's Lido. The *Lido* still operates on the Champs-Elysées as a supper club with an extravagant floorshow. Montreal's *Club Lido* hoped to share the glow of the Paris club. Despite the surrounding Depression, it was aimed at an upscale clientèle. It prided itself on beautiful décor, air conditioning, and top quality floorshows that changed frequently. There was a fine kitchen and the club offered all the latest cocktails and mixed drinks. The Art Déco-style exterior marquee was very distinctive, and it can still be seen on Stanley Street if you look carefully.

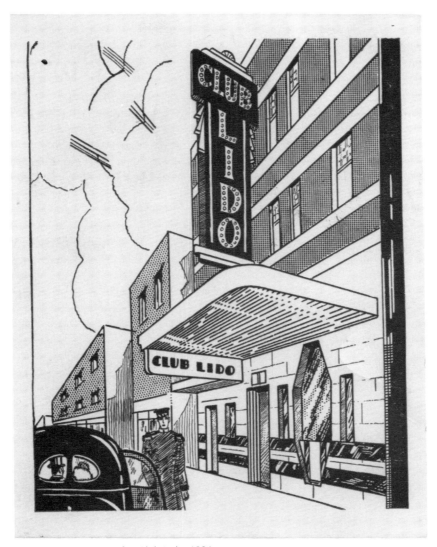

Promotional brochure for *Club Lido*, 1931
Joe Bell scrapbook, Concordia University Archives, 2.p13a

Club Lido, Easter 1935

The well-appointed facilities of *Club Lido* were previously occupied by the *Beaux Arts Cabaret* where Andy Tipaldi's Melody Kings had played in 1930. The *Tic Toc Club* was located on the ground floor of this large club, and it was one of the leading supper clubs in Montreal. In the 1930s *Club Lido* offered the latest cocktails, fine dining, dancing, and a floorshow. The club regularly prepared promotional brochures for special events like New Year's Eve and Easter.

The site would later be taken over by the *Chez Paree*. The club and casino that is currently on the same site is also called the *Chez Paree*.

Easter Greetings!

WITH A . . .

New Easter Revue

FEATURING
A GALAXY OF STARS

═══ AND ═══

AN ENTIRE NEW CHORUS OF
BROADWAY'S LOVELIEST GIRLS

─────

"A MUSICAL RIOT OF FUN"

─────

OPENING
EASTER MONDAY ~ APRIL 22ND
AT EIGHT O'CLOCK

The air conditioning system in the Club Lido is the only one of its kind in Canada. Installed by Kelvinator.

TABLE D'HOTE DINNER
DAILY 6 TO 10 P.M.

─────

The Beautiful Lounge
OPEN FROM 2 P.M.

★ ★ ★

DANCE TO THE STRAINS OF
CHARLES KRAMER'S ORCHESTRA

Promotional brochure for *Club Lido*, Easter 1935
Joe Bell scrapbook, Concordia University Archives, B.2p9a

Club Lido

Club Lido was an uptown nightclub with white entertainers and a white audience. It had a very active and ever-changing program of cabaret shows organized and produced by the renowned promoter/producers Fanchon and Marco, former cabaret dancers themselves. The shows featured dancers, novelty acts, and singers and they were beautifully staged. Musician Joe Bell (1908-72) played with the Charles Kramer Orchestra that was often the house band at *Club Lido*.

From 1945 to 1965 Bell played trombone with the Montreal Symphony Orchestra and he taught music at McGill University. During his career as a jazz musician Joe Bell kept a scrapbook of significant 1930s and 1940s Montreal nightclub memorabilia and clippings. The scrapbook includes many items from Club Lido. The Bell family deposited the scrapbook in the Concordia University Archives in 1987 and it has undergone conservation treatment.

Inside cover and page from promotional brochure for *Club Lido*,
September 30, 1935
Joe Bell scrapbook, Concordia University Archives, B.2p8

THE DINING ROOM — *The inspiration for its design and decoration are the beauty that is Venice. The atmosphere stimulates congeniality and hospitality. It has been praised as one of the most beautiful on the continent.*

THE COCKTAIL BAR AND LOUNGE — *It has been designed in spirit with the times. Its modern simplicity of decoration is a companion to any and all moods. Its subdued lighting and restful appointments are suggested of warmth and intimacy.*

Page from the promotional brochure for *Club Lido*, September 30, 1935
Joe Bell scrapbook, Concordia University Archives, B.2p8

Chef Nick Morara at Club Lido

Chef Nick (Narciso) Morara added to the panache and glamour of *Club Lido*. *Club Lido* was particularly proud of its ultra-modern facilities, including a large, streamlined kitchen. The menu included pricey items like filet mignon and lobster, and Morara's Italian specialties. At one time the kitchen also included Chef Jack Fong, who prepared Chinese specialties.

Morara was well known in Montreal's Uptown club scene. When he came to Canada from Bologna in 1922, he worked first at Roncarelli's restaurant near Windsor Station. When that closed he moved to Chez Ernest, a fancy Italian restaurant on Drummond north of Ste-Catherine Street. He went to *Club Lido* in the 1930s and stayed in that Stanley Street location through the early years of the *Chez Paree*. He was an accomplished chef who ran a good kitchen, but he was also congenial and sociable and mingled comfortably with the customers, offering personal attention and service. Morara was an early celebrity chef, and he was very much in demand. Although home base was *Club Lido* and later *Chez Paree*, he did some special stints at *Chez Maurice* and other nearby spots.

Carmen Miranda (1909-55) was born in Portugal and grew up in Brazil. She worked in a department store and as a seamstress, sang at parties, and even had a small hat-making business. In 1929 she recorded her first song, and quickly became a Brazilian super-star as a singer and in movies. She left for New York in 1939 where she appeared on Broadway to popular acclaim. She became a great success in American movies in which she sang and danced wearing the most extravagant costumes and headpieces, most of which she designed herself, and for which she became famous. Her singing, dancing and fabled costumes brought hot Latin style to many American movies of the 1940s. When her popularity in films waned in the late forties she joined the nightclub circuit with a very popular Latin act.

Chef Nick Morara with Carmen Miranda, 1948[?]
Nick Morara fonds, Concordia University Archives, P192-02-3

Dancers Stuart and Lea

Stuart and Lea appeared at *Club Lido* on several occasions in the 1930s. They were ballroom dancers with an act they performed in theatres and clubs. They were typical of the kind of act that appeared in Montreal nightclubs in the 1930s and 1940s.

Autographed publicity photograph of Stuart and Lea, January 1935
Joe Bell scrapbook, Concordia University Archives, B.1p38

Dedication reads: Hello Joe Hello! And Good Luck from Stuart and Lea,
Club Lido – January 22, 1935

Judy Kane

Judy Kane played at the *Bamboo Lounge* in 1948 and at the *Tic Toc* on Stanley a few months later. Her elegant costume and elaborate coiffure are typical of entertainers who performed in Montreal clubs in the 1940s.

Al Palmer (1913-71) was a police reporter, columnist, and writer-about-town who wrote for the *Montreal Herald*, the *Key West Citizen*, and the *Montreal Gazette*. He also wrote for magazines and published two books. From 1947 to 1969 Al Palmer wrote gossipy and colourful columns that chronicle the Montreal after-dark scene. Shirley O'Neil Marchessault donated Al Palmer's files to the Concordia University Archives in 1993. The files comprise scrapbooks containing all his published columns and articles, brochures and information related to his research and writing, and over 300 photographs related to his writing, many of them publicity photographs provided by entertainers visiting or performing in Montreal. Many of the photos are signed to Palmer with personal greetings.

Judy Kane was mentioned in several of Palmer's columns.

Al Palmer, date unknown
Al Palmer fonds, Concordia
University Archives,
P-084-02-332

Autographed publicity photograph of entertainer Judy Kane,1945[?] Photo: James Kollar Radio City, N.Y.
Al Palmer fonds, Concordia University Archives, P-084-02-10

Dedication reads: To Al, A sweet and wonderful guy, always be the best of friends Always, Judy Kane

The Kramer Dancers

This photograph illustrates typical glamorous costumes of the dancers who appeared in floorshows and as featured performers in Montreal nightclubs in the 1940s. It was one of the publicity photos found in the files of journalist Al Palmer, documenting Montreal nightlife beginning in the 1940s.

Publicity photograph of the Kramer Dancers, ca 1945 Photo: Gaby of Montreal
Al Palmer fonds, Concordia University Archives, P-084-02-01

Dedication reads: To Al Palmer With best wishes, "The Kramer Dancers"

Lili St. Cyr

Exotic dancer and striptease artist Lili St. Cyr was the darling of Montreal audiences at the *Gayety Theatre* from her first appearance there in March 1944.

The *Gayety* was the pre-eminent burlesque showcase in Montreal and Lili returned there many times. Many Montrealers (but not all) took her to their hearts and she remained a Montreal favourite until she retired from show business, and after. Quebec's Catholic clergy was outraged by Lili and her popularity and in 1951 she was charged with indecency (she was acquitted). Lili was born Willis Marie Van Schaack in 1913 in Minneapolis. She was raised by her grandparents, the Klarquists, and she was sometimes known as Marie Klarquist. She had no French connections and she did not speak French, but she adopted the stage name Lili St. Cyr. Her performances were original and artistic, with a particularly creative flair, and she was considered the "Queen of Strippers" in the 1940s and 1950s. Her act was sophisticated and always had a story line, in what was often described as an erotic ballet. She appeared in a number of movies, including "The Naked and the Dead" in 1958; there is even a passing reference to Lili in "The Rocky Horror Picture Show". She was married six times and when she retired she opened a lingerie business in Los Angeles. She died in seclusion in California in 1999. Montreal journalists often wrote about Lili and she became a friend of night beat columnist Al Palmer.

The *Gayety* was a burlesque theatre and it was the site of countless performances by both touring entertainers and Montreal acts. After renovations in the late 1950s, Gratien Gélinas used the theatre for his Comédie-canadienne theatre company, and in 1972 it became the home of *Théâtre du nouveau monde* (TNM), a leading Montreal theatre company. The TNM underwent extensive renovations in 1997.

Lili St. Cyr publicity photo. Photo: John E. Read, Hollywood
Al Palmer fonds, Concordia University Archives, P084-02-329

The inscription reads: To Al - From Lili and the swan!

Lili St. Cyr publicity photo. Photo: John E. Read, Hollywood
Al Palmer fonds, Concordia University Archives, P084-02-328

The inscription reads: To Al – with affection - Lily

The Johnny Holmes Orchestra at Victoria Hall

Trumpet player Johnny Holmes (1916-89) assumed the leadership of the Esquires in 1941, renaming it the Johnny Holmes Orchestra. Membership and size varied over the years but the band usually comprised between ten and twenty musicians. Holmes organized weekly dances for the band on Saturday nights between 1941 and 1950 at *Victoria Hall* on Sherbrooke Street West in Westmount. This dance band was much in demand in theatres and clubs, including *Chez Maurice* and the *Ritz-Carlton Hotel*. It was considered a breakthrough when the band's star black piano player, Oscar Peterson, played at the band's *Ritz-Carlton Hotel* booking. Most Montreal hotels, and especially the *Ritz*, admitted only whites.

Holmes returned to a day job in 1950 and the band broke up in 1951. Holmes assembled a part-time studio band that did CBC Radio broadcasts between 1959 and 1965, and he occasionally led big bands for radio, TV, and studio sessions until he retired in 1978.

The Johnny Holmes Orchestra on stage at *Victoria Hall*, 1943. On the left are vocalists Wally Aspell and Lorraine McAllister and featured piano player Oscar Peterson. Photo: News Pictures of Canada
Johnny Holmes fonds, Concordia University Archives, P016-01-86

Oscar Peterson

The Johnny Holmes Orchestra played capacity weekly Saturday night dances at *Victoria Hall* between 1941 and 1950. They also played other dates as a whole or in groups. The band rehearsed regularly at *Victoria Hall*. Pianist Oscar Peterson joined the band in 1942 and remained as featured soloist until 1947.

Oscar Peterson was born in Montreal in 1925. He studied music and played as an amateur. As an adolescent, he did radio appearances on CKAC, CBM, and CBC. During the time he was with the Holmes band he made other appearances and more than twenty recordings with RCA Victor in Montreal. In 1948 Peterson left the Holmes band and led a trio at the *Alberta Lounge* (near Windsor Station), frequently sitting in after hours with Louis Metcalf's International Band at *Café St. Michel*, a few blocks away. Norman Granz featured the star Montreal piano player in a 1949 Jazz at the Philharmonic Concert at Carnegie Hall in New York City and Peterson went on to a stellar international career in jazz.

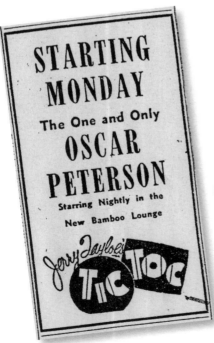

Press clipping,
The Montreal Standard,
October 8, 1949
Meilan Lam fonds,
Concordia University Archives,
P135

Rehearsal of the Johnny Holmes Orchestra at *Victoria Hall*, 1945[?]
Johnny Holmes fonds, Concordia University Archives, P016-02-70

Russ Dufort (left) on drums, Oscar Peterson on piano

Alys Robi

Alice Robitaille was born in 1923 in Quebec City, where she sang in public from a very early age. She came to Montreal when she was 12 to study singing and dancing, and soon changed her name to Alys Robi. She began her career as a pop singer in1937, in the well-developed Montreal entertainment scene that included night clubs, theatres, radio broadcasting, and the recording industry. Alys quickly became a Montreal singing star at the *Monument National* on the lower Main, St-Laurent Boulevard. She performed on Gratien Gélinas' CKAC program "La Veillée du samedi soir", and later on "Tambour battant" as well as on CBC Radio in Toronto. Her first hits were recorded with Lucio Agostini and had a Latin flavour. She began an international career, and was acclaimed in New York and London. On the brink of a Hollywood breakthrough, in 1948 she suffered a nervous breakdown and was hospitalized for five years. She made a comeback in Montreal in 1953 at the *Casa Loma* and the *Montmartre* and other Montreal clubs but she suffered discrimination after her mental illness and never again achieved her former success. There was a revival of interest in Alys Robi in the 1990s, and one of her big hits, "Tico-Tico" (1945), is still remembered very fondly.

The *Monument National* was built in 1893 by the Société St-Jean-Baptiste. The space hosted lectures, plays, operettas, comedy and musical revues, and was briefly a cinema. It was the home of Yiddish theatre in Montreal for nearly fifty years. In its heyday it was an important Montreal venue for performers like Emma Albani and Édith Piaf. It was in serious decline by 1965 when Canada's National Theatre School rented the space for public performances; they bought the building in 1978. One of the oldest operating theatres in Canada, the *Monument National* was restored for its centenary in 1993.

Press clipping,
The Montreal Standard,
February 14, 1948
Meilan Lam fonds,
Concordia University Archives,
P135

Autographed photograph of singer Alys Robi, September 1947
Photo: Bruno of Hollywood NYC
Al Palmer fonds, Concordia University Archives, P084-02-25

Dedication reads: Dear Al. With many thanks for all your help.
Best Wishes from Alys

"You Belong to My Heart", sheet music with image of Alys Robi.
Montreal, 1941, Canadian Music Sales Corp. Ltd.
Alex Robertson collection, Concordia University Archives, P023-S-0402

"Tico-Tico", sheet music. Montreal, 1943, Canadian Music Sales Corp. Ltd.
Alex Robertson collection, Concordia University Archives, P023-S-0055

Rockhead's Paradise

Former porter and smuggler of bootleg liquor Rufus Rockhead bought the three-storey *Mountain Hotel* at Mountain and St-Antoine in 1928. The hotel had a tavern and a long, narrow cocktail bar on the ground floor, a beverage room on the second floor, and hotel rooms on the third floor. He opened *Rockhead's Paradise* in 1931 when he brought in American black entertainers. He soon enlarged the club by cutting an oval hole in the third floor so it was possible to look down at the second-floor stage. Rockhead was an affable host who wore a red rose in his lapel. He built a reputation for friendly hospitality and top-quality black entertainment—*Rockhead's* was famous for its black entertainers, although clients were both black and white. Like most clubs, Rockheads survived through the popularity of their feature-act floorshows. The house band played the music for the shows and for dancing.

Rockhead had liquor licence problems in 1937 and again between 1953 and 1962 when only the tavern was open. In 1977 the building was sold, *Rockhead's* was closed, and the *Rising* Sun briefly moved into the space. The building was demolished in 1980.

Staff at *Rockhead's Paradise*, 1946[?] Photo: Émile of Montreal
John Gilmore fonds, courtesy Walter Bacon, Concordia University Archives, P004-02-44

Standing, from left: Lena Welch (bar girl), Rose Bryant, unknown, unknown, Barbara Crawford Pucci (hat check girl).
Sitting, from left: Lucille Wade (cigarette girl) and unknown.

Café St. Michel 1947

In 1934 the *Monte Carlo Grill* opened on Mountain, just south of St-Antoine. It soon became *Ideal Gardens*, and finally *Café St. Michel*. *Café St. Michel* was across the street from *Rockhead's Paradise*, which was on St-Antoine at the corner of Mountain. Mountain and St-Antoine came to be known as "The Corner", a Montreal jazz legend. "The Corner" was home to some of the most exciting jazz in the city, and it was a trendy club destination for many years.

Louis Metcalfe's International Band put *Café St. Michel* on the map when it was the house band there between 1946 and 1949. The Metcalfe band was one of the early mixed race bands in Montreal. It featured local musicians with various ethnic backgrounds, thus the name, the International Band. This is the band that introduced be-bop to Montreal audiences. The band played be-bop at afternoon rehearsals, between shows, and after hours when other musicians came to jam and to listen to the music. When they were in town, jazz musicians like Duke Ellington sat in with the band after hours and Oscar Peterson was a frequent visitor when he finished his own performances. Local fans and tourists from Canada and the U.S. flocked to hear the musicians experimenting with this exciting new musical expression and *Café St. Michel* thrived. The International Band composition changed during its existence (1946-50) but the most stable players were Metcalfe, Willy Girard, Herb Johnson, Al King, Steep Wade, and Willie Wilkinson. The band and the club remain a Montreal entertainment legend.

SOUVENIR of Café St. MICHEL

St Michel

Located at 770 Mountain Street just below St. Antoine. Cafe St. Michel is in the heart of Montreal's Harlem section and is known from coast to coast as The Cafe famous for the finest colored shows in Montreal. There is an early show and a late show every night with continuous dancing to Louis Metcalfe, his trumpet and his orchestra.

Fully licensed under the liquor laws of the Province of Quebec, Cafe St. Michel boasts one of the finest bars in downtown Montreal and all drinks are sensibly priced.

We appreciate your patronage and hope you call again. If you would like to send a souvenir of your visit to Cafe St. Michel to a friend simply fill in the address on the back of the card and your waiter will be glad to have it mailed for you.

M. Turgeon
President

Café St. Michel

Cover and inside spread of a souvenir postcard of *Café St. Michel*, April 1947
Herb Johnson fonds, Concordia University Archives, P088/2B

LOUIE METCALF
and his
INTERNATIONAL BAND
present a three in one Jam Session
at
CAFE ST. MICHEL
every Sunday afternoon from 3.30 to 7 p.m.

One hour and a half Jazz Concert and
one hour and a half of dancing and floor show.

Every night Cafe St. Michel presents floor
shows at 11 and 1.15
Saturday night, 9, 11 and 1.15

Canada's Greatest Jazz Band

The Show-Shops

There is no novelty in Negro and White Musicians making good music together, but when a group of seven men representing that many different nationalities are playing terrific jazz in a Montreal night-club, Brother, - that's news.

The combo that has been playing since the beginning of the year at the Club St. Michel is fronted by Louis Metcalf, veteran of the Ellington, Armstrong, Fletcher Henderson, Joe "King" Oliver and Basie Bands.

DOWN BEAT - William Brown-Forbes

Just about a year ago famed jazz trumpeter Louie Metcalf came to Montreal from New York to fulfill an engagement with his band, found he couldn't bring his musicians with him. So he studied the local jazz field and found that he didn't need to worry. In a short time he came to the Cafe St. Michel with one of the finest small band aggregations to be heard in this country.

MONTREAL STANDARD - KEN JOHNSTONE

The St. Michel Band has got the knack of producing some of the best jazz heard in this burg in many a year. If you like that kind of stuff, just drop in and forget about the rest of the goings on. It may be a smart idea for the management to sponsor Sunday afternoon Jam sessions there.

MONTREAL HERALD - AL PALMER

Canadian Jazz is getting some stiff Jazz in the arm these days. Biggest hypo is the new seven piece combo of Louis Metcalf playing the Club St. Michel in Montreal.

DILLON O'LEARY - TORONTO

It isn't the type of music that Metcalf's men about-tune make that brings this ork into the unusual class, it is the heterogeneous nationalities of its members. Each of the seven musikers is of a different origin and each is a master of his profession. Look over this list of personnel and you'll get an insight into the reason Louie has dubbed his band "Democracy in Music"

Louie Metcalf, (Negro Cherokee), maestro.
Herb Johnson, (Negro American) Tenor Sax.
Harold Steep Wade, (Canadian West Indian) Piano.
Al King, (Negro Mexican), Bass.
Mark Wilkie Wilkinson (Swedish) Drums.
Butch Watanade, (Japanese Canadian) Trombone
Willy Girard (French Canadian) Violin.

William Brown Forbes - Toronto

L'Orchestre du Café St-Michel, sous la direction de Louie Metcalf, fournit de l'excellente musique.

Roland Cote - Le Canada

At Cafe St. Michel where Louie Metcalf and his band give out with some very creditable jazz can be found such connoisseurs as Bob Harvey and Oscar Peterson.

Kay Sisto - Radio World

Autograph

CANADA'S GREATEST JAZZ BAND

Butch Watanade

Steewade

Herb Johnson

Louie Metcalf

LOUIE METCALF
AND HIS INTERNATIONAL BAND

Willy Girard

Wilkie Wilkinson

Al King

Autographed Souvenir Program
of Louie Metcalf (sic) and his International Band, 1947[?]
Herb Johnson Fonds, Concordia University Archives, P088/2B

Café St. Michel

For most nightclubs glamorous dancers in a chorus line were an integral part of the floorshow that attracted audiences. Dancers Tina Baines, Bernice "Bunny" Jordan and Marie-Claire Germaine were part of one of the earliest chorus lines of all-Canadian black dancers at *Café St. Michel* in the 1940s when Louis Metcalf's International Band was the house band. These dancers and other local black dancers like Olga Spencer had worked individually and in chorus lines that were composed mostly of American dancers. But until "Frenchie" Mendez put the group together and did their choreography, when they wanted a black chorus line Montreal clubs had imported most of the dancers from Harlem.

Café St. Michel and *Rockhead's Paradise* were downtown clubs at what became famous as "The Corner", close to where the black community lived, and to the trains where many blacks worked as porters. At "The Corner" black entertainment was the drawing card, but both black and white audiences were welcome.

Dancers at *Café St. Michel*, 1946[?]. Photo: Émile of Montreal
Tina Brereton fonds, Concordia University Archives, P074-02-04

Left to right: Tina Baines (Brereton), Bernice Jordan (Whims), and Marie-Claire Germaine (Maurice)

Jan Savitt Orchestra at the Auditorium

The *Auditorium* was a large licensed dance hall in the 1940s. It had earlier been the *Roseland Ballroom*. At the time of this photo Jan Savitt's swing band was the headliner and the house band was Stan Wood's big band.

Jan Savitt Orchestra playing at the *Auditorium*, later the site of the *Bellevue Casino*, 1945[?]
John Gilmore fonds, Concordia University Archives, P004-02-155

Bellevue Casino

In 1949 Harry Holmok opened the *Bellevue Casino* on the site of the former *Auditorium* and the *Roseland Ballroom* on Ontario (now President Kennedy) near Bleury. The *Bellevue Casino* was a large three-floor operation with a ground-floor lounge. The shows changed frequently, the entertainment was mostly American headliners, and there was always a good chorus line. Bix Belair led the house band that played for dancing between shows. Best of all, the drinks were inexpensive. The *Bellevue Casino* was big; it was cheap; it was fun; and it was a big success, especially with young people looking for a good time that was within their means. The *Bellevue* and other large clubs were geared to high volume. When Mayor Jean Drapeau's clean-up after 1954 led to police raids, strict enforcement of closing time, and other things that had never been very important in Montreal, attendance dropped and the whole scene became threatened. The *Bellevue Casino* closed and the building was demolished in September 1962 when Ontario Street was widened.

Flower Girl Marian at the *Bellevue Casino* selling white gardenias for $2 each, as she appeared in a spread on Montreal nightlife in the *Montreal Standard*, April 28, 1951

Nick Morara fonds, Concordia University Archives, P192

Press clipping, *The Montreal Standard*, April 16, 1949
Meilan Lam fonds, Concordia University Archives, P135

Vic Vogel, Oliver Jones, and Bruce Parent at the Montmartre Cabaret, 1951

In the early 1950s the *Montmartre* left its original location at Ste-Catherine and Clark, and moved around the corner to St-Laurent, site of the former *Frolics* and of *Connie's Inn* in the 1930s. These musicians were out on the town on their night off from an engagement at another club.

In the 1940s Pax Plante and Jean Drapeau worked for reform of a corrupt municipal infrastructure. Freewheeling Montreal clubs started feeling the pinch when Drapeau was elected mayor in 1954. Closing times and other regulations were enforced as they had never been enforced in the clubs before, and there were frequent police raids. As pressure increased, tensions surfaced between rival underworld factions, and in 1955 the *Montmartre* and other clubs were attacked and demolished by gangs. The raids and violent struggle between the gangsters drove away the customers, but this was not the only cause for concern. In the 1950s, times were hard for the clubs as audience tastes and habits changed, and commercial television entered the picture. Many people stayed home, glued to their television screens.

Young musicians Vic Vogel, Oliver Jones, and Bruce Parent at the *Montmartre Cabaret*, 1951
John Gilmore fonds, Concordia University Archives, courtesy Oliver Jones, P004-02-86

Montreal Post-War: A Smorgasbord of Clubs

There were many clubs in post-war Montreal, and until television beamed entertainment into everyone's living room, the crowds came to dine, dance, and be entertained. Each club had its own style and atmosphere so you could choose a spot where you might be a regular and be well known, or a place with a favourite band or a special headliner. Some clubs were very large like the Bellevue Casino (near Bleury) or El Mocambo out east on Iberville and others were more intimate or had special features. The choices were many.

The Stork Club had been around from the late 1930s. This was one of the many Montreal night spots that were named for famous clubs in New York or Paris. It was named for one of the most famous nightclubs of all, New York's Stork Club, the quintessential New York nightclub on East 53rd Street that opened in the 1920s and closed in the mid-sixties. It featured food as well as floorshow entertainment and dancing. It was the site of the 1945 movie of the same name, and the club in the 1950 movie "All About Eve" is the Stork Club's Cub Room. Montreal's Stork Club was a popular and glamourous club that was just north of Her Majesty's Theatre. It had an elegant white interior, a very long bar, a dance floor and a band, but no floorshow. It went into decline in the 1950s and closed in the 1970s.

In its heyday the *Chez Paree* was a Montreal hot spot-a place to see and be seen when there were hundreds of clubs scattered throughout the city. The club offered service and entertainment in the grand style of the day, and it took many service staff to run the operation. Chef Nick (Narciso) Morara wrote in Italian on his copy of the publicity spread opposite: "This is the cabaret where I work, and these are all the employees."

Staff of *Chez Paree* as they appeared in a spread on Montreal nightlife in the *Montreal Standard*, April 28, 1951.

Nick Morara fonds, Concordia University Archives p192

Chez Paree

The upscale *Chez Paree* took over the site of *Club Lido* on Stanley Street in the 1950s. The well-known Montreal gambler Harry Ship was the owner. There was a lounge next door, an elevator took patrons to the second floor, and the shows were top headliners like Frank Sinatra. Several bands were going in various parts of the large club, including the Black Magic Room. The *Chez Paree* was a supper club and there was dancing and good food. The menu featured charcoal grilled fish, steak, chicken and chops but they also had a good selection of Jewish deli specialties and sandwiches.

As the 1950s progressed, the morality squad continued to clamp down on the clubs, commercial television and rock music had a growing stranglehold on entertainment, underworld violence escalated, and attendance at the clubs decreased dramatically. *Chez Paree* and all the clubs struggled. The glitz and glamour that had marked the nightclubs of the 1930s and 1940s disappeared. By 1960 *Chez Paree* was a strip joint. An era had ended.

Chez Paree menu cover 1955[?]
Herb Johnson fonds,
Concordia University Archives,
P088/2B,2

FONTAINE BLEUE *à la carte menu*

Appetizers

CHOPPED LIVER	.60
EGG PLANT	.60
ICRA	.60
PICKLED PIKE	.60
BAKED CARP	.60
ASSORTED HORS-D'OEUVRES	.75
PETZA	.60
GEFILTE FISH	.60
PICKLED HERRING	.60
CREAMED HERRING	.60
SCHMALTZ HERRING	.60
KISHKA	.60
SHRIMP COCKTAIL	1.00

Soup

SOUP DU JOUR	.35

Entrées

INDIVIDUAL DORE (BROILED)	2.50
BROILED HALIBUT	2.50
BROILED SALMON	2.50
CHARCOAL BROILED RIB STEAK	3.25
CHARCOAL BROILED T-BONE STEAK	4.00
CHARCOAL BROILED SIRLOIN STEAK	4.00
CHARCOAL BROILED CHOICE FILET MIGNON	4.00
MINCED SIRLOIN STEAK	2.25
CHEZ PAREE MIXED GRILL	3.25
PEPPER STEAK A LA CHEZ PAREE	3.00
HALF CHICKEN-IN-A-BASKET	2.75
CHARCOAL BROILED CHICKEN	2.75
CHARCOAL BROILED DUCKLING	2.50
BROILED LAMB CHOPS	3.25
CHARCOAL BROILED SWEETBREADS	2.50
BREADED VEAL CUTLET	2.75
LIVER STEAK-N-ONIONS	2.25
KARNATSLACH	2.25
COMBINATION SALAD	2.25

[ALL MEATS ARE THE FINEST PRIME RED BRAND]   [ABOVE ORDERS INCLUDE ALL TRIMMINGS]

Side Orders

(6) VARENIKAS .75	(6) LATKAS .75	(6) KREPLACH .75
SOURS (ASS'T.) .50	CHEF SALAD .50	VEGETABLES .35

Desserts

FRUIT CUP .40	FRENCH PASTRY .40	STEWED FRUITS .40	ICE CREAM .40

Beverages

COFFEE .25	TURKISH COFFEE .25	TEA .25	MILK .25

Sandwiches

BACON AND TOMATO	1.00
HAM AND CHEESE	1.00
CHOPPED LIVER	1.00
SALAMI (ITALIAN)	1.00
WESTERN	1.00
CHICKEN	1.25
CLUB SANDWICH	1.50
HOT CHICKEN	1.50
HOT BEEF	1.50
STEAK SANDWICH	2.50

Chez Paree menu, inside spread 1955[?]
Herb Johnson fonds, Concordia University Archives, P088/2B,2

Esquire Club

The *Esquire Club* on Stanley south of Ste-Catherine was one of the popular uptown clubs in Montreal during the 1940s and early 1950s. It opened in 1940 and during World War II it was a favourite unlicensed supper club and dance club for servicemen and their guests. After the war owner Cleaver took Norm Silver as a partner. The young Silver had been a partner in *Miss Montreal*, a trendy diner on Decarie not far from *Ruby Foo's*. They closed the *Esquire* temporarily, re-designed the club, and re-opened as the *Esquire Show Bar* in 1951. Its central feature was a long bar around a raised stage, and continuous performance. Patrons could have dinner, dance, enjoy a chorus line, and watch a floorshow that would include a variety of acts such as comedians, singers, novelty dancers, or jugglers. The food was good and was not too extravagantly priced, in the tradition of the original *Club Esquire*. The *Esquire Show Bar* brought in headliners like Peggy Lee, Edie Gormé, Duke Ellington, Count Basie, and Dean Martin. A nightly radio interview show was hosted from the lounge area. The changes kept the customers coming for a number of years but business started dropping off by the mid-fifties, as it did all over Montreal, and elsewhere. The *Esquire* introduced rock 'n' roll in 1956 and they had success cultivating the youth market.

There were problems with the *Esquire* liquor licence, resulting from a 1963 charge of toleration of prostitution. The *Esquire* fought the ruling and got public support. After operating for six months without a licence attendance figures were catastrophic. The *Esquire Show Bar* closed in December 1972.

Press clipping, *The Montreal Standard*, April 16, 1949
Meilan Lam fonds,
Concordia University Archives,
P135

Menu a la Carte

APPETIZERS AND RELISHES

Hors d'Oeuvres, $1.25   Canape of Caviar, $1.00   Paté de foie gras, $1.00
Canape Russe, 75c   Canape of Sardine, 75c
Fillets d'Anchovy on Toast, 75c   Oysters on Half Shell, Half Doz., 75c
Stuffed Celery Roquefort, 75c   Queen Olives, 75c   Stuffed Olives, 75c
Ripe Olives, 75c   Mixed Olives, 75c   Hearts of Celery, 50c
Lobster Cocktail, 85c   Shrimp Cocktail, 85c   Crab Meat Cocktail, 85c
Sea Food Cocktail, 85c   Grape Fruit Supreme, 40c   Fruit Cocktail, 40c
Tomato Juice Cocktail, 35c

SOUPS

Onion Soup au Gratin, 75c   Green Turtle Soup, 75c   Consomme au Crotons, 50c
Consomme Julienne, 50c   Consomme with Sherry, 65c
Cream of Tomato, 50c   Chicken Broth with Rice, 50c

EGGS AND OMELETTES

Virginia Ham Steak with Fried Egg, $1.00   Breakfast Bacon with Fried Eggs, 85c
Shirred Eggs, 60c   Eggs Vienna, 75c   Scrambled Eggs, 60c
Poached Eggs on Toast, 60c   Ham Omelette, 85c   Cheese Omelette, 85c
Plain Omelette, 65c   Jelly Omelette, 75c   Parsley Omelette, 75c
Esquire Special Omelette, $1.00   Omelette with Chicken Livers, $1.00
Omelette with Mushrooms, $1.25

FISH AND DEEP SEA FOOD

Fried Deep Sea Scallops, Tartar Sauce, $1.00
Broiled Lake Trout, Maitre d'Hotel, $1.00   Fried Fillet of Sole, Tartar Sauce, $1.00
Fried Oysters with Bacon, $1.00   Baked Oysters a La Casino, $1.00
Oysters Baltimore, 90c   Oysters Stewed in Cream, $1.00
Shrimps Newburg, $1.25   Crab Meat au Gratin, $1.25
Lobster in Season — Thermidore, $1.50; Newburg, $1.50
Half Broiled Live Lobster, $1.25

ENTREES AND SPECIALS

Chicken en Casserole Jardinière, $1.75   Chicken à la Maryland, $1.75
Fried Breast of Chicken, $1.50   Chicken à la King, $1.50
Half Fried Young Chicken, $1.25   Chicken Livers en Brochette, $1.25
Sweetbreads with Mushrooms and Bacon en Brochette, $1.25
Sweetbreads under Glass, $1.25   Fresh Mushrooms with Bacon on Toast, $1.00

FROM THE GRILL

Planked Steak per Person, $2.50   Broiled Fillet Mignon, $1.75
Fillet Mignon with Fresh Mushrooms, $2.00   Single Sirloin Steak, $1.50
Double Sirloin Steak, $2.75   English Mixed Grill Esquire, $1.50
Half Broiled Chicken, $1.25   Calves Liver with Bacon, $1.00
Broiled Lamb Chops, $1.25   Grilled Ham Steak Hawaiian, $1.00

VEGETABLES

New Green Peas, 45c   Fresh String Beans, 45c   Fresh Spinach, 40c
Carrots Vichy, 35c   Fried Egg Plant, 40c   Small Green Asparagus Tips, 50c
Brussels Sprouts, 45c   Braised Onions, 40c   French Fried Onions, 50c
Broccoli, Hollandaise, 60c   Cauliflower, Hollandaise, 50c
Cauliflower au Gratin, 50c

POTATOES

Plain Boiled, 25c   Home Fried, 30c   French Fried, 35c
Long Branch, 40c   Julienne, 40c   Lyonnaise, 40c
Hashed Brown, 35c   Au Gratin, 50c   Fried Sweet Potatoes, 40c
Candied Sweet Potatoes, 50c

Menu a la Carte

COLD MEATS WITH JELLY OR POTATO SALAD

Cold Roast Beef, 90c   Jellied Ox Tongue, $1.00   Sliced Breast of Chicken, $1.25
Virginia Ham, $1.00   Assorted Cold Cuts, $1.25

RAREBITS AND SPAGHETTI

Welsh Rarebit, 85c   Golden Buck, $1.00   Scotch Woodcock, $1.00
Yorkshire Buck, $1.25   Melted Canadian Cheese on Toast, 85c
Spaghetti with Meat Balls, $1.00   Spaghetti Caruso, $1.25
Spaghetti au Gratin, $1.00   Spaghetti with Chicken Livers, $1.25
Spaghetti Italian, $1.00

SALADS

Lobster Salad, $1.25   Crab Meat Salad, $1.25   Shrimp Salad, $1.00
Chicken Salad, $1.25   Tuna Fish Salad, 75c   Tomato Surprise, 85c
Hearts of Lettuce, 75c   Lettuce and Tomato Salad, 85c   Waldorf Salad, 90c
Combination Salad, 90c   Fruit Salad, 90c   Vegetable Salad, 90c
Either Mayonnaise or French Dressing served with Salads.
Thousand Island Dressing, 25c   Russian Dressing, 35c
Roquefort Dressing, 40c extra

SANDWICHES

Sandwiches served on Whole Wheat or White Bread
Toasted Sandwiches 10c extra
Virginia Ham, 50c   Jellied Tongue, 50c   Special Club, $1.00
Chicken, 75c   Swiss Cheese, 50c   Pate de foie Gras, 75c
Lettuce, Tomato and Bacon, 75c   Imported Sardine, 50c   Salmon, 45c
Lettuce and Tomato, 50c   Chicken Salad Sandwich, 65c
Western Sandwich, 60c   Assorted Sandwiches, 85c per Person

CHEESE

Imported Swiss Cheese, 45c   Imported Camembert, 45c
Imported Roquefort, 50c   English Stilton, 50c
Imported Gruyere, 45c   Imported Oka, 40c   Kraft Cheese, 30c
Cream Cheese, 40c   Old Canadian, 40c

DESSERTS

Assorted French Pastry, 35c   Coupe St. Jaques, 50c   Coupe Esquire, 75c
Peach Melba, 50c   Parfait au Rhum, 60c   Sliced Pineapple, 35c
Preserved Beckwith Figs, 40c   French Pancakes with Red Currant Jelly, 65c
Banana Fritters, 60c   Pineapple Fritters, 60c
Pear Fritters, 60c   French Toast, 65c
Vanilla Ice Cream, 30c   Chocolate Ice Cream, 30c   Strawberry Ice Cream, 30c

BREAD AND TOAST

Plain Toast, 25c   Buttered Toast, 25c   Cinnamon Toast, 35c
Melba Toast, 40c   Milk Toast, 50c

BEVERAGES

Pot of Tea, 25c   Pot of Coffee, 25c   Demi Tasse, 20c
Glass of Milk, 15c   Hot Chocolate, 30c   Malted Milk, 40c

Extra Service Charge of 50c for 1 order serving two persons.
Children under 10 years of age half price for Table d'Hote Meals
Dishes not on this menu served upon request.
Cover Charge Commences at 9.00 p.m.
The Rumba Room is open for private parties Monday till Thursday inclusive, with or
without Refreshments being served.   Menus and prices quoted upon request.
The management of Club Esquire reserves the right to place a service or damage charge
upon any person or party at their own discretion.

Esquire Club menu, 1945[?]
Joe Bell scrapbook, Concordia University Archives, B.2p69

Sophie Tucker

Sophie Tucker was famous for being "The Last of the Red Hot Mamas". She was born in Russia but grew up in Connecticut. She joined a burlesque show with a ragtime repertoire in 1908 and briefly appeared with the Ziegfeld Follies. She played the theatre and club circuit in North America and in England and was a great audience favourite, adding jazz and ballads to her routine. She emphasized her "fat girl" image. She had a powerful voice and her act was geared to adult cabaret audiences, with much suggestive innuendo and humour. Tucker also made movies and appeared regularly on radio, and later on television. She died in 1966.

Sophie Tucker played in Montreal on a number of occasions, doing a show at the *Orpheum* as early as 1917. She appeared at the *Loew's* in 1932, and she signed copies of her Feist sheet music at Simpson's Department Store.

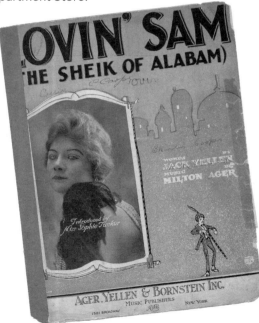

"Lovin' Sam (The Sheik of Alabam)",
sheet music with an image of Sophie Tucker.
New York, 1922, Ager, Yellen & Bornstein Inc.
Alex Robertson collection,
Concordia University Archives,
P-23-S-1053

Sophie Tucker publicity photo, 1940[?]. Photo Maurice Seymour, Chicago
Nick Morara fonds, Concordia University Archives, P192-02-1

The inscription reads:
To Nick from Sophie Tucker

It was signed to Nick Morara, the chef at Club Lido and later Chez Paree.

Maury Kaye

Maury Kaye was born Morris Kronick in Montreal on March 29, 1932. He died in Montreal on February 3, 1983. He came from a musical family. He began piano lessons at six years of age and went on to study at the Conservatoire de Musique de Montréal, and then at McGill University. He taught himself trumpet and he also played the clarinet. Kaye conducted the house band at *El Morocco* in Montreal in its heyday from 1952 to 1959 and he was very well known to Montreal clubgoers. He accompanied many headliner singers who came to Montreal, including Tony Bennett, Pearl Bailey, Édith Piaf, Sammy Davis Jr., Josephine Baker, and Mel Tormé. He also led his own band, which played upstairs at Dunn's Restaurant. His career was interrupted by heroin addiction. He travelled between Montreal and Toronto between 1960 and 1975 during a time when the club scene was changing dramatically and work was often scarce. Back in Montreal in 1975 he worked with trumpet player Charles Ellison, singer Barbara Reney, and many others, often playing at the *Rising Sun*.

THE "Maury Kaye" QUARTET

Gaby

Publicity photo for Maury Kaye quartet, 1951,
used for an engagement at the *Esquire*. Photo Gaby.
John Gilmore fonds, courtesy Rebecca Kronick,
Concordia University Archives, P004-02-114

El Morocco

In its heyday Montreal's *El Morocco* was one of the best clubs in town. It was a large and successful operation. It shared the name of the Manhattan club with the famous zebra-stripe banquettes, where celebrity photographers snapped socialites and movie stars for the New York gossip columns. *El Morocco* was where you headed for a special night out on the town. There were excellent floorshows with appearances by well-known entertainers, along with an accomplished chorus line. Maury Kaye led the house band through most of the 1950s. You could always have a nice meal. As the club situation deteriorated generally in the late 1950s it became increasingly difficult to support headline acts and attendance spiraled downward. Norm Silver bought *El Morocco* and for a brief time there were small-scale productions of Broadway shows.

El Morocco was in three separate locations in Montreal. The first, operated by Dave Bernie, was located at 1433 Mansfield Street, a building that had housed the *Washington Club*, the *Embassy*, the *Golden Dome*, the *Cavendish*, and the *Silver Slipper*. The next *El Morocco* was at 1410 Metcalfe at Ste-Catherine Street. The third location was 1445 Closse Street, opposite the Montreal Forum. *El Morocco* was partially demolished to build a bank and the remaining site later became *Norm Silver's Mustache*, with a Dixieland theme. It too closed in the 1970s.

El Morocco postcard
Al Palmer fonds, Concordia University Archives, scrapbook, July 23, 1955

The Chic'n Coop

The *Chic'n Coop* was owned by the Hill brothers — Eli, Cecil, and Victor. It was strategically located on the south side of Ste-Catherine between Drummond and Stanley. It was around the corner or a short hop across the back lane from the *Lido* and its *Tic Toc Club*, and later the *Chez Paree*. During World War II, *Club Lido/Chez Paree* chef Nick Morara organized the opening of the *Chic'n Coop*. It was close to the downtown business and shopping area , as well as many other Montreal nightclubs. It became an after-hours gathering place for entertainers and was famous for its chicken and spare ribs. The *Chic'n Coop*'s upstairs *Indian Room* was decorated with paintings of Natives of the Blackfoot tribe, and it was set up for dining and dancing. The neon sign was a Ste-Catherine Street beacon. When Frank Sinatra appeared at *Chez Paree* in 1953 he went out clubbing after the show with impresario Jimmy Nichols and his wife Norma Hutton, feature vocalist at the *Normandie Roof*. In the early hours of the morning they went to the *Chic'n Coop* before heading back to the *Mount Royal Hotel*.

The *Chic'n Coop* was located in the home built in 1864 for Thomas D'Arcy McGee (1825-68), journalist, poet, Father of Confederation and Irish patriot. McGee was assassinated in Ottawa in 1868. The house had lintel stones decorated with carved shamrocks, but they were covered by the extension that brought the building flush with Ste-Catherine Street and created the *Chic'n 'Coop*, and its Indian Room. The building was destroyed by fire in November 1962, but the lintel stones were recovered, and the Hill brothers donated them to Loyola College where they were placed on the Loyola campus. They have recently undergone conservation treatment and the McGee lintel stones will soon be installed in the new Concordia complex at Guy and Ste-Catherine, not far from their original location.

Montreal singer Norma Hutton with Frank Sinatra at the *Chic'n Coop*, February 1953. Alan Hustak fonds, Concordia University Archives, P191-02-01

Lion d'or

The *Lion d'or* opened in 1930 on Ontario east at Papineau, and for three decades it was a vibrant part of Montreal's club life. Stars like Alys Robi and Peggy Lee were featured at the club. It was always a cabaret, with a master of ceremonies introducing local and visiting entertainers. In the 1950s the *Lion d'or* went into decline and by the 1970s the club went dark. Like so many others it succumbed to changing public tastes and social conditions and an anti-vice crusade in the city. Fortunately the building was not torn down and the place was not gutted and replaced with a modern restaurant or tavern—the fate of so many other clubs.

The building was bought by the owners of the "Au petit Extra" restaurant that is next door to the club, and in 1987 they undertook to revive the *Lion d'or*. They did a major facelift to make the building usable for current needs, and restoration work continues as funding becomes available. The *Lion d'or* now looks much like it did in the 1930s and the lights are on again. The *Lion d'or* is one of the few old-style nightclubs in Montreal that have succeeded in re-inventing themselves, and it is now a venue for receptions and special events.

Au Lion d'or—Cabaret—1676 rue Ontario Est, Montréal, Canada.

Postcard of the *Lion d'or*, 1930[?]
Herb Johnson fonds, Concordia University Archives, P088/20-postcards

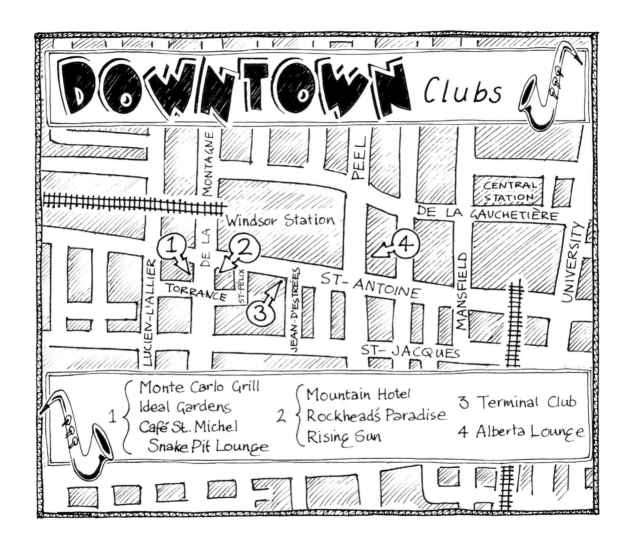

DOWNTOWN Clubs

1
- Monte Carlo Grill
- Ideal Gardens
- Café St. Michel
- Snake Pit Lounge

2
- Mountain Hotel
- Rockhead's Paradise
- Rising Sun

3 Terminal Club

4 Alberta Lounge

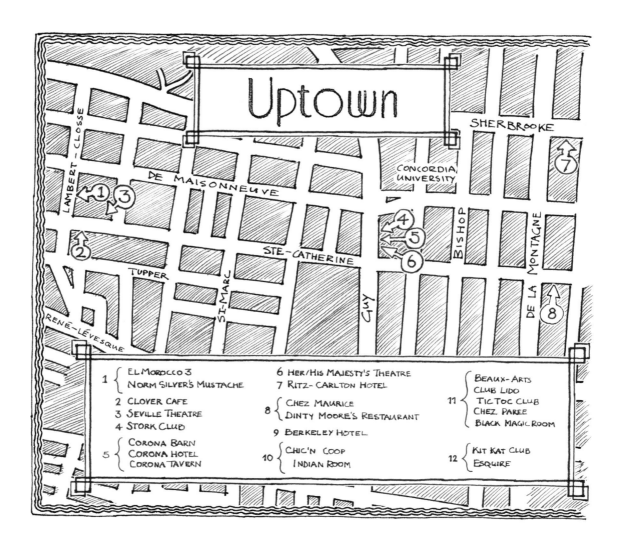

Uptown

1 { EL MOROCCO 3
    NORM SILVER'S MUSTACHE

2 CLOVER CAFE
3 SEVILLE THEATRE
4 STORK CLUB

5 { CORONA BARN
    CORONA HOTEL
    CORONA TAVERN

6 HER/HIS MAJESTY'S THEATRE
7 RITZ-CARLTON HOTEL

8 { CHEZ MAURICE
    DINTY MOORE'S RESTAURANT

9 BERKELEY HOTEL

10 { CHIC'N COOP
     INDIAN ROOM

11 { BEAUX-ARTS
     CLUB LIDO
     TIC TOC CLUB
     CHEZ PAREE
     BLACK MAGIC ROOM

12 { KIT KAT CLUB
     ESQUIRE

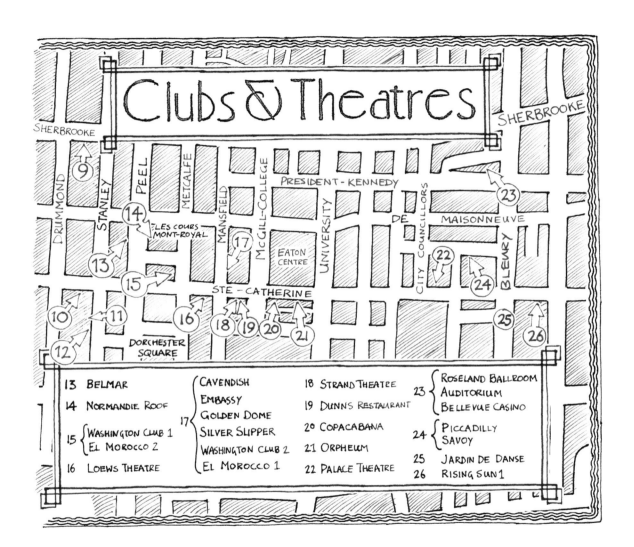

Clubs & Theatres

13	BELMAR	18 STRAND THEATRE	23 { ROSELAND BALLROOM / AUDITORIUM / BELLEVUE CASINO
14	NORMANDIE ROOF	19 DUNNS RESTAURANT	
15	{ WASHINGTON CLUB 1 / EL MOROCCO 2 }	20 COPACABANA	24 { PICCADILLY / SAVOY }
16	LOEWS THEATRE	21 ORPHEUM	25 JARDIN DE DANSE
		22 PALACE THEATRE	26 RISING SUN 1

17 { CAVENDISH / EMBASSY / GOLDEN DOME / SILVER SLIPPER / WASHINGTON CLUB 2 / EL MOROCCO 1 }

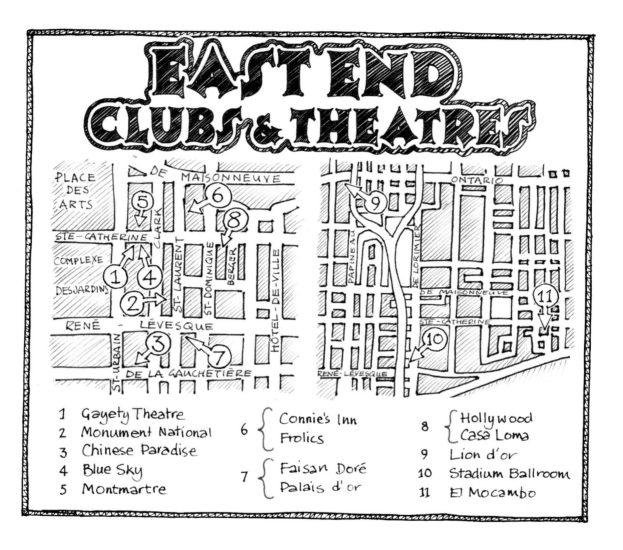

EAST END CLUBS & THEATRES

1 Gayety Theatre
2 Monument National
3 Chinese Paradise
4 Blue Sky
5 Montmartre

6 { Connie's Inn
    Frolics

7 { Faisan Doré
    Palais d'or

8 { Hollywood
    Casa Loma

9 Lion d'or
10 Stadium Ballroom
11 El Mocambo

Clubs, Lounges, Dancehalls and Theatres Mentioned in this Book

Alberta Lounge
de la Gauchetière Street and Peel Street (present site of Château Champlain)

Auditorium
(also site of **Bellevue Casino**)
375 President-Kennedy Avenue, north side, just west of Bleury Street

Bamboo Cage/Bamboo Lounge
Stanley Street

Beaux Arts
(also site of **Club Lido** and **Chez Paree**)
1258 Stanley Street

Bellevue Casino
(also site of **Auditorium**)
375 President-Kennedy Avenue, north side, just west of Bleury Street

Belmar
1424 Peel Street

Berkeley Hotel
1188 Sherbrooke Street West, south side, between Stanley and Drummond streets

Black Magic Room
(with **Chez Paree**)
1258 Stanley Street

Blue Sky
65 Ste-Catherine Street West

Café St. Michel
(also site of **New Ideal Gardens** and **Monte Carlo Grill**)
770 de la Montagne Street, just south of St-Antoine

Casa Loma
94 Ste-Catherine Street East

Cavendish
(also site of **Washington Club, Embassy, Golden Dome, El Morroco** and **Silver Slipper**)
1433 Mansfield Street

Chez Maurice/Chez Maurice Danceland
1244 Ste-Catherine Street West

Chez Paree
(included **Black Magic Room**)
(also site of **Beaux-Arts** and **Club Lido**)
1258 Stanley Street

Chinese Paradise (Grill)
57 de la Gauchetière Street

Clover Café (Club)
2204 Ste-Catherine Street West, south-east corner of Lambert-Closse

Club Lido
(also site of **Beaux-arts** and **Chez Paree**)
1258 Stanley Street

Connie's Inn
(also site of **Montmartre** and **Frolics**)
1411-1417 St-Laurent Boulevard

Corona Barn/Corona Hotel/Corona Tavern
1431 Guy Street

Dinty Moore's Restaurant
(downstairs from **Chez Maurice**)
1244 Ste-Catherine Street West

El Mocambo
Iberville near Ste-Catherine

El Morocco
First location – 1433 Mansfield Street
(also site of **Washington Club, Embassy, Golden Dome, Cavendish,** and **Silver Slipper**)
Second location – 1410 Metcalfe Street at Ste-Catherine
Third location – 1445 Lambert-Closse Street
(became **Mustache, Norm Silver's Mustache** and **My Father's Mustache**)

Embassy
(also site of **Washington Club, Golden Dome, Cavendish, El Morocco** and **Silver Slipper**)
1433 Mansfield Street

Frolics
(also site of **Montmartre** and **Connie's Inn**)
1411-1417 St-Laurent Boulevard

Gayety Theatre
Ste-Catherine Street West at St-Urbain Street

Golden Dome
(also site of **Washington Club, Embassy, Cavendish, El Morroco,** and **Silver Slipper**)
1433 Mansfield Street

Her/His Majesty's Theatre
1421 Guy Street near Ste-Catherine

Hollywood
92 Ste-Catherine Street East

Jardin de Danse
Bleury Street below Ste-Catherine Street West

Loew's Theatre
Ste-Catherine Street West, south side, west of Mansfield Street

Mountain Hotel
(also site of **Rockhead's Paradise** and **Rising Sun**)
1258 St-Antoine Street West

Monte Carlo Grill
(also site of **New Ideal Gardens** and **Café St. Michel**)
770 de la Montagne Street just south of St-Antoine Street

Montmartre
First location - 59 Ste-Catherine Street West at Clark Street
Second location – 1411-1417 St-Laurent Boulevard
(the second location was also the site of **Frolics** and **Connie's Inn**)

Monument National
West side of St-Laurent Boulevard between René-Lévesque Boulevard and Ste-Catherine Street

Mustache
(also known as **Norm Silver's Mustache** and **My Father's Mustache**)
(also site of **El Morocco**)
1445 Lambert-Closse Street, near Ste-Catherine

My Father's Mustache
(also known as **Mustache** and **Norm Silver's Mustache**)
(also site of **El Morocco**)
1445 Lambert-Closse Street near Ste-Catherine Street

New Ideal Gardens
(also site of **Monte Carlo Grill** and **Café St. Michel**)
770 de la Montagne Street just south of St-Antoine Street

Norm Silver's Mustache
(also known as **Mustache** and **My Father's Mustache**)
(also site of **El Morocco**)
1445 Lambert-Closse Street near Ste-Catherine Street

Normandie Roof
Top floor of Mount Royal Hotel, now Les Cours Mont-Royal on Peel Street, between de Maisonneuve Boulevard and Ste-Catherine Street

Orpheum Theatre
South side of Ste-Catherine Street near University Street

Palace Theatre
South side of Ste-Catherine Street West between University Street and McGill College Street

Rising Sun
First location - South side of Ste-Catherine Street near Jeanne-Mance
Second location - 1258 St-Antoine Street West (also site of **Mountain Hotel** and **Rockhead's Paradise**)

Ritz-Carlton Hotel
1228 Sherbrooke Street West

Rockhead's Paradise
(also site of **Mountain Hotel** and **Rising Sun**)
1258 St-Antoine Street West

Roseland Ballroom
First location – Phillips Square
Second location – 375 President-Kennedy Avenue

Savoy
1457 St-Alexandre Street at Mayor Street

Silver Slipper
(also site of **Washington Club**, **Embassy**, **Golden Dome**, **Cavendish**, and **El Morocco**)
1433 Mansfield Street

Stadium Ballroom
Corner of Réné-Lévesque Boulevard East and De Lorimier Street

Stork Club
1433 Guy Street

Strand Theatre
912 Ste-Catherine Street West
(at Mansfield, south-east corner)

Terminal Club
1114 St-Antoine Street West
(across from Windsor Station)

Tic Toc Club
1258 Stanley Street

Victoria Hall
4626 Sherbrooke Street West near Lansdowne Street, Westmount

Washington Club
First location – 1004 Mount Royal Place
Second location – Ste-Catherine Street West and Metcalfe Street
Third location – 1433 Mansfield Street (also site of **Embassy**, **Golden Dome**, **Cavendish**, **El Morroco**, and **Silver Slipper**)

Wood Hall
Unknown location

Bibliographic Information

Archival Materials

For more than twenty years the Concordia University Archives staff has gathered information about Montreal jazz and the clubs and other venues in which it has been played.

I have made use of many parts of the Archives holdings in the preparation of this book. The images used in the book are from the Archives. I have made extensive use of the following to help describe the materials clearly and to put them into context:

The John Gilmore fonds – P004

I have used some of the audio taped interviews that John Gilmore did in preparation for his books on Montreal jazz history, *Swinging in Paradise: The Story of Jazz in Montreal* (1988) and *Who's Who of Jazz in Montreal: Ragtime to 1970* (1989). These books have been extremely valuable sources of information to many researchers and they have been helpful to me as well. I have also consulted the photographs in the fonds and have found the author's information about them to be extremely helpful.

The Joe Bell fonds – P010

The Joe Bell scrapbooks have been a major source of documentation and information about Montreal nightlife in the 1930s and 1940s. The Bell family has been helpful in providing additional information about Joe Bell's career.

The Johnny Holmes fonds – P016

Band leader Johnny Holmes gathered together his archives as a Montreal band leader and deposited them in the Archives in 1986. Until his death in 1989 he visited many times and spent long hours carefully identifying photographs and explaining their circumstances. Johnny cared a great deal about his band and the musicians he played with over so many years and he wanted to be sure that all his musicians got the credit they deserved. Many family members of band members have visited the Archives and consulted the materials, as have a wide variety of other researchers.

The Clyde Duncan fonds – P018

Clyde Duncan was a member of Mynie Sutton's Canadian Ambassadors band, and he also played with Herb Johnson. The fonds has helped my understanding of the Montreal music scene of the 1940s.

The Myron Sutton fonds – P019
The Mynie Sutton scrapbook provides rare and priceless documentation of the life of a black bandleader in Montreal in the 1930s and early 1940s. Mynie's family has provided additional stories and information about him and his career.

The Alex Robertson collection – P023
Alex Robertson did extensive research on musical activity in Montreal between 1913 and 1970. The Archives has created an events database with this information and it is an important reference tool that I have used a great deal. Robertson also amassed an important collection of early recordings pressed in Montreal by the Berliner and Compo recording companies. He also collected sheet music and many other materials that have all proven very useful in piecing together the whole entertainment scene in Montreal.

The Bob Redmond fonds – P064
 Bob Redmond played in, and was press agent for, the Johnny Holmes band. His photographs and notes about his music career help document the big band era in Montreal.

The Tina Brereton fonds – P074
Tina's photographs of the glamour girl dancers at Café St. Michel are a treasure, and Tina's conversations and ongoing interest in the Archives have been enormously helpful to me.

The Vic Vogel fonds – P082
Vic Vogel has been depositing his materials in the Archives for many years. His legendary storytelling about the Montreal music scene during off-the-cuff visits to the Archives has been a great source of information. Vic has also generously answered many questions and dug out information when it was needed.

The Al Palmer fonds – P084
Al Palmer's scrapbooks contain all his writing during his long journalistic career. Al wrote gossipy columns that contain valuable snippets of information and colourful details about Montreal nightlife between 1940 and 1971.

The Herb Johnson fonds – P088
Herb Johnson kept much documentation during his long career as a jazz musician. His fonds has helped me understand many aspects of the Montreal music scene.

The Meilan Lam fonds – P135

Meilan Lam worked for many years doing wide-ranging research for her wonderful 1998 National Film Board film, *Show Girls*. The film chronicles the lives of three women who danced in Montreal night clubs in the 1940s: Tina Baines Brereton, Benice Jordan Whims, and Olga Spencer Foderingham. Meilan has generously shared both her knowledge and research materials with many other researchers. Her press clippings have been extremely useful to me. Meilan's encyclopedic knowledge of the local scene has been the subject of many conversations since she began her research in the Archives and she is an unfailing source of reliable information and clear insight.

The Nick Morara fonds – P192

Norma Morara Hayes generously shared information about her father's long career in Montreal restaurants and nightclubs. She recently deposited the documentation in the Archives. It sheds light on the clubs from the perspective of a well-known non-musician personality who was an intimate part of the club scene.

Websites

I am grateful for the detailed information on the Berliner and Compo recording companies that is available on the Library and Archives Canada's excellent web site dealing with Canada's history of sound recordings, *The Virtual Gramophone* is a multimedia site about the early years of Canadian recorded sound. It has images, audio, biographies of musicians, and a great deal of historical information. This site is an important resource and it can be found at:

http://www.collectionscanada.ca/gramophone/m2-3000-e.html

The information on Canadian broadcasting history on the Canadian Communications Foundation website, *The History of Canadian Broadcasting*, has also been helpful. It can be found at:

http://www.broadcasting-history.ca/

The *Massicotte Albums* are available on the website of the Bibliothèque nationale du Québec. They document Montreal streets as well as social, cultural and economic activity, between 1870 and 1920. These materials have been very helpful to my understanding of Montreal and how it has developed. The albums can be found at:

http://www.bnquebec.ca/massic/accueil.htm

Archives staff have consulted many web sites over the years to collect further information about individual entertainers, venues, and events. These are too numerous to mention, but they often include the official website of an entertainer, group, or venue.

Newspapers
I have frequently established or confirmed dates by going back to newspapers from Montreal and elsewhere. I have also consulted a great number of newspaper clippings from our archival holdings.

Books
I have consulted the following books:

Gilmore, John. *Who's Who of Jazz in Montreal: Ragtime to 1970*. Montreal: Véhicule Press, 1989. This is a valuable source of information about Montreal musicians.

Gilmore, John. *Swinging in Paradise: The Story of Jazz in Montreal*. Montreal: Véhicule Press, second printing 1999. Gilmore's groundbreaking history is an important source of information about the Montreal music scene.

Lanken, Dane. *Montreal Movie Palaces: Great Theatres of the Golden Era 1884-1938*. Waterloo, Ontario: Penumbra Press, 1993
This is a stunning book on Montreal theatres and it contains reliable and well-organized information about Montreal movie theatres.

Miller, Mark. *Such Melodious Racket: The Lost History of Jazz in Canada 1914-1949*. Toronto: The Mercury Press, 1997. Mark Miller's book is a significant addition to the literature on Canadian jazz history.

Vipond, Mary. *Listening In: The First Decade of Canadian Broadcasting 1922-1932*. Montreal & Kingston: McGill-Queen's University Press, 1992. This is one of the bibles of Canadian broadcasting.

Weintraub, William. *City Unique; Montreal Days and Nights in the 1940s and '50s*. Toronto: McClelland & Stewart Inc. 1996. Bill Weintraub's personal recollections of Montreal in the 1940s and 1950s were both informative and entertaining, and provided valuable insight into the period.

Acknowledgements

Special thanks go to all those who have taken the care to create, collect, and preserve materials, and particularly to the many people who have donated them to the Concordia Archives so we can all share them for generations to come.

An archivist's thank you goes to the photographers acknowledged in the book and to all the anonymous photographers whose photos the Concordia Archives cherishes and preserves. Special thanks go to John Gilmore for his careful research and especially for the taped audio interviews he did with so many people involved with the Montreal jazz and club scene. These interviews provide precious and irreplaceable information that we might not have otherwise.

My thanks go also to the many people who have answered questions, searched their memory or their files, and provided many different kinds of information, especially Alan Hustak, Len Dobbin, Meilan Lam, Vic Vogel, Mary Vipond, Tina Brereton, and Norma Hayes, the daughter of Nick Morara.

I also wish to acknowledge the staff of the Concordia University Archives who made important contributions to the preparation of this book: Nathalie Hodgson, Vincent Ouellette, Caroline Sigouin, Kiki Athanassiadis, Stanley Clarke, Josh Cuppage, Ahmad El Sidani, and especially Bruce Henry who helped me avoid many pitfalls.

Jennifer Clare Pearson and Oisin Little responded with good humour and great style to a rush request for maps. John Stewart made it all look good.

Thanks to Simon Dardick for his customary patience, encouragement, and understanding.

All the photos and graphic materials in this book are in the Concordia University Archives.

Index

Page references to
illustrations are in italics.

Stepping Out, The Golden Age of Montreal Night Clubs was designed by J.W.Stewart.
The text is set in Avenir. Titles are set in Blue Boy and Elegiac which are adaptations of typefaces
made especially for this book by Mr. Stewart. Pre-production for the book and cover was done by
Infoscan Colette and the book was printed by AGMV-Marquis Inc.
on 100 lb. Productolith Matte paper.